Galway Women in the Nineteenth Century

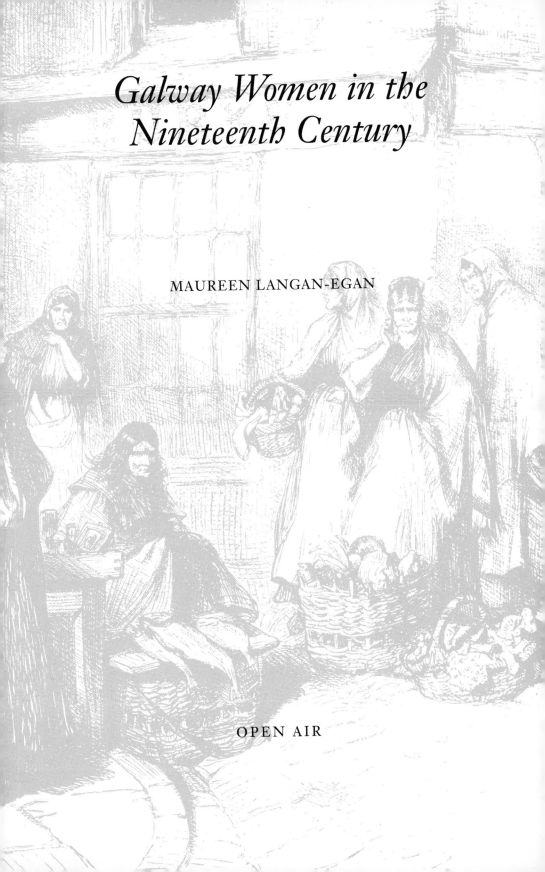

Galway Women in the Nineteenth Century

MAUREEN LANGAN-EGAN

OPEN AIR

Published by
OPEN AIR
an imprint of Four Courts Press
Fumbally Lane, Dublin 8, Ireland
Email: info@Four-Courts-Press.ie
and in the United States for
FOUR COURTS PRESS
c/o ISBS, 5804 N.E. Hassalo Street, Portland, OR 97213.

© Maureen Langan-Egan 1999

A catalogue record for this title is available from the British Library.

ISBN 1-85182-461-8

This book was set in 10.5 on 14 pt Janson by
Carrigboy Typesetting Services, County Cork.
Printed in Ireland by
ColourBooks Ltd, Baldoyle, Dublin.

Contents

PREFACE   7

INTRODUCTION   9

1   *The Necessities of Life*   15
    Employment   15
    Housing   25
    Clothing   36
    Food   43

2   *The Nature of Society*   53
    Marriage   53
    Unmarried Mothers   61
    Widows   67
    Religion   75
    Education   85

3   *Distress*   108
    Distress and Famine   108
    Migration and Emigration   129
    Women and Crime   135

EPILOGUE   147

NOTES   155

SOURCES   157

LIST OF ILLUSTRATIONS   160

INDEX   161

SPECIAL ACKNOWLEDGEMENT

This publication was grant-aided by the Publications
Fund of National University of Ireland, Galway.

Preface

I wish to acknowledge my debt of gratitude to many people, without whose aid this book would not have been completed. In its original form, this work was submitted as a PhD dissertation; however, it has been revamped with a view to publication. The late great Professor T.P. O'Neill first inspired me to undertake the study of women's lives and for that I am particularly grateful; thanks also to the staffs of the Libraries of the National University of Ireland, Galway, Trinity College, Dublin and Galway County Library, especially Mary Kavanagh, Maureen Moran and Peter Corley; to the National Archives, National Museum and National Libraries, the Dublin Diocesan Archives; to Marie Mannion of the Galway Family History Society for her guidance; to the Mercy Sisters in Galway, Loughrea, Tuam, Clifden, Gort and Portumna, and to the Presentation Sisters of Galway and Tuam for original material; to the parish priests of Galway City parishes and Dunmore, Claregalway, Moycullen for access to parish records; to the Revd Anthony Previte for access to Church of Ireland records for Roundstone, Moyrus, Clifden and Omey; to Barbara Page-Hanify of Lindfield, New South Wales, for her assistance with Australian source material, in particular that relating to her distant relative, M.J. Hanify; to Dr Caitriona Clear of the National University of Ireland, Galway and Dr J.J. Lee of University College Cork for assistance in locating research material. It was my great good fortune to have had Dr Brian Austen as my Director of Research; his guidance was invaluable.

I am especially grateful to Mr Michael Adams of Four Courts Press for his comments and assistance, and for undertaking the publication of this work.

Finally, I am indebted to my sons Bernard and Gerard, and especially to my husband Bernard, for his great patience, while this work was being completed. I owe much to the women of Galway, whose story this is. Mo mhíle buíochas daoibh go léir.

Introduction

Ireland was relatively prosperous in the early part of the nineteenth century because of the high prices available to Irish farmers for agricultural products, but the period from 1815 up to 1845 or thereabouts has been rightly described by one commentator as a 'true Thirty Years War to the Irish people, a struggle between their vital needs and the interests of landlords and money-lenders'. The most basic causes of Irish poverty in this century were rapid population growth, low productivity in tradeable goods and over-reliance on the potato. From the 1820s onwards, the country was badly affected by structural unemployment and a great decline in the level of industry, which caused great poverty, as many of those employed in industry, at least part-time, were farmers and women. As women's incomes contributed greatly to family well-being, female unemployment depressed family incomes to a dangerously low level, particularly in subsistence areas, such as large parts of County Galway, which did not have improving landlords, migrant labour or remittances from emigrants.

The destruction of the textile industries affected Galway, a noted 'yarn county', very badly. Flax, in particular, was a very useful crop on small pieces of ground; no tithes were payable to the Established Church on income from its sales, and it was easier to spin than wool. 'Bandle-linen' (a poor-quality fabric) was widely made. Landlords had distributed spinning wheels *(tuirní)* and reels in Connacht, either free of charge or for a minimum charge. Their motives were not altogether altruistic, for it was reported that 'the women in many families spin more than the whole amount of the house and gardens', which means that the income earned from spinning was greater than that earned from the produce of the gardens and the earnings of other family members; thus, landlords were assured of their rents. The linen industry declined after 1815, which marked the end of the Napeolonic Wars. As regards woollen goods, Ireland had been able to supply its requirements in 1800, but by 1830 the industry was in 'terminal decline'; tariffs were lifted in 1826, allowing cheaper imports.

This sharp decline in cottage industry reduced the demand for labour and increased disguised unemployment. This loss of supplementary income made it more difficult for tenants to pay high rents, yet many continued to do so, by selling illicit spirits and reducing living standards. For some, this meant that 'potatoes were eaten at every meal, and through all seasons of the year'. While households became destabilized because of the decline in domestic industry, a residual knowledge of skills remained, which was used by relief organisations to provide permanent relief during the Great Famine.

Many of Ireland's difficulties were caused by an agricultural system which before the Famine was disorganised and badly balanced. The conacre system of renting land was a major cause of poverty and tension in the countryside. There was very little agricultural machinery, and much tillage was carried on by the intensive use of the spade, particularly in growing potatoes on the misnamed 'lazy-bed' system, which involved five times as much labour as ploughing and was 'a massive soak for surplus or under-employed labour'. Such work took place on small holdings in the West of Ireland, where over 60% of the holdings were between one and five acres in 1841. Families living on such holdings constituted a type of 'dual economy', which consisted of subsistence crops and fuel and cash crops. Worse off were the landless and near landless labourers and cottiers, who lived a very precarious existence; to a great extent, they were trapped by an over-dependence on the land. However, some farmers got involved in the sale of butter, fresh eggs and slaughtered meat to industrial

1: Eyre Square, the 'heart of Galway': a busy Fair Day scene

cities of England; in this they were greatly assisted by the
development of coach roads, railways and steamship services.

For the population at large, income per capita was growing
very slowly, towns which might have provided employment were
not developing as rapidly as might have been expected, there was
a conservative approach to the introduction of new technologies,
and 'whatever progress there was, was too little, too slow and too
unevenly spread', particularly in the West of Ireland, where
Galway, the second largest county in Ireland, is situated.

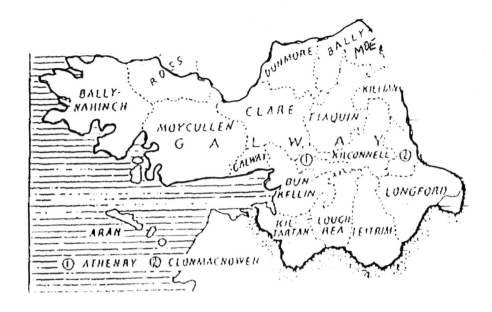

2: A map of Galway showing the baronies,
after Edwards, *An atlas of Irish history*

In Ireland in the nineteenth century, as well as 32 counties, there were four cities and three towns administered as counties; the latter included Galway, often referred to as 'The City of the Tribes'; in this book, it will be called Galway City, its more usual name. County Galway consists of one and a half million acres, of which 77,922 are under water, including 150 lakes, the largest of which is Lough Corrib, which almost divides the county into two largely contrasting regions. The population of County Galway and Galway City recorded in the Censuses was as follows:

POPULATION

Year	County	City
1821	309,599	27,775
1831	381,564	33,120
1841	422,923	17,275
1851	297,897	23,787

The sharp decline in the prosperity in Galway City in the decade 1831–41 was caused by unemployment and high mortality, caused by a severe cholera epidemic in the early part of the decade.

Galway City was an important port. In pre-Famine times, 86% of its exports consisted of corn, meal and flour, while tobacco formed 21% of its imports; it also had an important fish market. Potatoes, pigs and poultry formed the staples of the West. Athenry and Tuam were corporate and statute towns, both having received royal charters; but they were in decline for much of the century. Ballinasloe was noted for its traditional horse fair, held in October. Towns such as Loughrea, Eyrecourt, Gort and Headford functioned as market towns. They also had newly founded post offices as did many lesser towns in the county such as Dunmore and Craughwell. New towns were set up for specific purposes, in Roundstone, to foster fishing; in Clifden, to provide jobs, a task made easier by the development of main roads through Connemara and along the coast, which helped develop a growing tourist industry and inspired many visitors to write of their travels. Of one such travel writer, it was said: 'Like so many tourists of the period, Curwen was inspired by the landscape and troubled by the people'. The obvious misery of a large number of the people troubled many visitors. In Connemara, such misery was very visible along the coast with its tiny holdings and crowded population, contrasted with the more sparsely populated inland areas. Visitors to towns were forcibly struck by the evidence of poverty: Asenath Nicholson, a famous American Quaker visitor, was astounded, when she found on a visit to Clifden in May 1845, that there had been no bread in the town for six weeks. She asked how it was possible when 'there had been no failure of crops, in an assize town (which would be assumed to be fairly prosperous) that people had lived for six weeks on nothing but potatoes'. Many commentators saw the lack of employment as a major cause of Irish poverty; however, while the Irish were stereotyped as being 'lazy wretches, who prefer beggary to work', the fact is that many of them spent their lives in an unremitting search for paid work and in unremitting toil (often unpaid) in an effort to survive.

I

The Necessities of Life

EMPLOYMENT

Unemployment and underemployment were endemic in Ireland in the 1830s and 40s, particularly in agriculture. Much agricultural underemployment was linked to very small holdings and the lack of capital investment, which was necessary as landlords in Ireland rented the bare soil to their tenants. Torrens, a famous economist of the time, argued that the want of combined labour and capital on the land was the cause of the low effective power of the agricultural industry in Ireland. However, the movement towards consolidation of holdings had already begun after 1815. Laws, such as the Sub-Letting Act of 1826, accelerated the process, causing more evictions and unemployment in the short term. The post-Famine change in the pattern of agriculture from tillage to livestock farming also caused unemployment, affecting both men and women. Moreover, jobs in this sector available to women were seasonal and poorly paid, and were often given to men, even though they were usually paid more. As demand for these positions outpaced supply, some unscrupulous employers used this to depress agricultural wages. The number of women employed in agriculture was limited by the number of employers who could pay for such hired help, and, as servants were frequently fed by the employers, they were frequently let go, when food supplies, particularly potatoes, became scarce.

Women undertook all kinds of agricultural work, particularly in the 'throng' or 'hurry' seasons (spring and autumn); they saved hay, bound corn and picked potatoes all over the county; in some

3: A Galway fishwife

4: 'Feamainn Bhealtaine': seaweed was valued as fertilizer

districts, such as Clonfert, they also 'footed turf'. Women also worked on their family holdings, particularly when their menfolk had migrated or emigrated. Widows, especially those with young children, encountered particular difficulties when seeking agricultural employment. Many prospective employers, unless motivated by charity, were unwilling to employ a widow with young children as they would incur extra costs in feeding them. As jobs became scarcer, women sought alternative sources of independent

[17]

income. Of necessity, these involved employment which did not require much cash or expertise. Some began to huxter and deal in fruit and turf. The 1851 Census recorded 56 female turf dealers in County Galway, where none had been so employed in 1841. Several women began to sell eggs, which had previously been used as food in the hometeads; others began to sell poteen.

To compound the misery general in the country, cottage industry was also in decline and, except for the North-East of the country, there were no factories to take up the slack. The Famine delivered a final crippling blow to Irish industry. Whereas the weaving industry had declined earlier, now the spinning of wool, cotton and linen failed causing a dramatic drop in the numbers of women employed between 1841 and 1851. In 1841, women carders in Galway numbered 477 adults and 53 under the age of fifteen. By 1851, this number had been reduced to 129, with none under 15. In fact, the main source of independent income enjoyed by women all but vanished. The measure of their loss can be gauged by the fact that wives used frequently pay the rent by the produce of their spinning flax and knitting stockings. The post of lodging house keeper became popular. In 1851 in County Galway there were 35 female lodging house keepers and ten male; in the city, 10 female and 4 male. This position was popular among widows. In the circumstances of the time, it was a relatively well-to-do woman who had a house and furniture who could earn her living in this way. Usually, this was an urban occupation as in the country it was usual for poor travellers to obtain lodgings free. By 1851, women had succeeded in obtaining some posts in medicine. In this year, there were 82 nurse tenders in the county and seven in the city, as well as 22 midwives. Nurse tenders were sometimes employed by people who had a surplus of cash, if a family was stricken with fever or other illness. By a savage irony, the Famine which wrecked the livelihood of so many women also created some employment opportunities. The post of wardmaid was developed in the temporary fever hospitals and did not disappear after the Famine. A few women achieved the position of matron in the public institutions, a post which was comparatively well paid. In 1851, there were three gaol matrons in the city of Galway and 27 matrons in various public institutions in the county, whose duties included elementary instruction of female prisoners in reading and writing.

Positions as teachers in the primary schools were much sought after. The feminisation of the teaching profession took place against the force of public opinion, which in general regarded teaching as a male profession, as revealed by the fact that the teacher-proprietors of the hedge schools were mainly male. The early Commissioners of National Education shared this viewpoint, declaring their intention to use female teachers only for sewing or knitting or plaiting straw or 'other female work'. In private schools, the public attitude was sometimes reflected in the wages teachers could command, when payments from parents were the norm. It was also reflected in the fact that no female inspectors had been appointed by 1851. We will discuss teachers' salaries and working conditions in our discussion of Education.

Positions in government departments were eagerly sought after because they offered regular salaries and a degree of respectability. In the Post Office, in particular, in the 1850s, there were almost as many postmistresses as postmasters in Galway County. In the commercial world, several women opened small stores and were appointed agents for the sale of coffee and tea.

Along the coast, women took an active part in fishing: they turned flax into yarn and also spun hemp for the fishing nets; sometimes, they took part in fishing operations, working on the oyster beds in Ballynahinch along with the men; in the Claddagh, they baited hooks on spilliards. When fishermen returned to port, the wives and children disentangled the lines and tied up the hooks ... to the top of the snouding. Most fishmongers were female, outnumbering males by approximately seven to one both in the city and county in 1851, selling their husbands' catch or hawking fish bought from the boats.

One of the few growth areas in employment, for both men and women, after the Famine up to 1881, was domestic service, regarded as a respectable calling by parents, since servants were

a Claddagh boy making twine

5: 'Rags seem the refuse of a sheep.' Sir Walter Scott

provided with room and board. This applied also to governesses. Domestic service was one of the jobs which was divided along the lines of gender, religion and education. In 1871, for instance, most of the people employed in domestic service in Galway City were Roman Catholic, two-thirds of whom could neither read nor write. Such figures reveal the extent of cultural deprivation at the lowest point of the social scale, even though universal primary education had been available since 1831. In the early years of the national school system, however, small fees were payable, which many poor parents could not afford.

Women who could read and write were enabled thereby to obtain better positions. One such was the post of shop assistant, which was becoming popular with the growth of the retail trade. Innkeepers, hoteliers and publicans could read and write, unlike many of the lodging-house keepers. The *Galway Vindicator* of 15 February 1850 specified that the Head Nurse to be appointed to the Workhouse Infirmary must be 'well able to read and write'.

In general, single women or widows were appointed to official positions. The one exception to this general policy was in the workhouses, where preference was frequently given to a master and matron who were married to each other. Joseph Burke, a Poor Law Commissioner, felt that the couple's interest was a spur to good management: 'When they are not husband and wife, continual boils [arguments] take place.' However, the Commissioners in general did not approve of children; in 1843, annoyed by the presence of officers' relatives, both near and distant in the workhouses, they asked Assistant Commissioners to use their advice and influence to secure the appointment of officers 'unencumbered with families'.

The extent of chronic unemployment and underemployment is particularly difficult to quantify. The records of public institutions and census figures for beggars and vagrants reveal the extent of female unemployment and destitution. In 1851, in both County Galway and Galway City, the numbers of female beggars outnumbered males by about five to one. In the workhouses, ablebodied women, most of whom were unable to obtain work, consistently outnumbered unemployed able-bodied men.

Begging was rampant. Referring to Galway City, Osborne stated:

> I can only suppose that the opportunity of begging of the many men earning good wages and the cheapness of coarse fish has drawn hither the masses of nearly naked women and children who by day choke up every thoroughfare.

In Galway in 1871, only in two of the public institutions (the jails) listed for 'Galway and Town,' did males outnumber females. This showed a continuation of a pattern revealed in 1851, which mirrored the situation all over Ireland. This position pertained despite the best efforts made by women to find new sources of independent income. Some adapted to changing adverse circumstances by trading, generally as hucksters (huxters), selling fruit, fish, crockery. Several had 'standings' at fairs and markets. A 'standing' could range from a basket displaying wares to a large stall; it was said that many a splendid fortune had been commenced in them. Trading in eggs, fish and poultry developed.

While some women sold poultry raised on their own holdings, others acted as middlemen. Dutton noted six women 'forestallers' in the Galway market who frequently bought up fowl to retail again in the same market. Poultry raising could present some difficulties; in some parts of Connacht, women were forbidden by their landlords to keep fowl as 'trespassing fowl would damage crops'.

Several women adapted to the changing pattern in agriculture. In 1851, there were 59 adult females and 97 young girls under the age of fifteen employed as herdswomen. This marked a new development. In the textile industry, some spinners began to execute 'sewed muslin work' (a new category in the 1851 Census) but this work came to an end in 1857 because of the financial crisis in the USA, the main market for this product. Other women combined trades: several women, who dealt in poultry, were also spinners and, although neither calling provided much income, they allowed the women involved to contribute substantially to the household.

Emigration was a recourse frequently used by those not on the lowest grade of poverty and 'who viewed themselves as self-sufficient beings with an economic role to play in their families and communities', a role increasingly being denied them in Ireland. A total of 24,868 men and 25,970 women are recorded as having emigrated from County Galway in the decade 1851–61, approximately 70% of them in the first few years. Those who remained adopted a variety of strategies to obtain employment against overwhelming odds, not always successfully.

Unemployment in the long term caused many undesirable effects. In the earlier part of the century, the economic role of women was important at all levels of society, but 'most crucial perhaps at the level closest to subsistence'. At that time, the economic contribution of women was so essential to the family that they enjoyed economic independence. With economic recession, the reduced earning power of women tilted the balance of economic power within the family in favour of the male. This change, which affected not only a woman's independence and her marriage prospects, was a relevant factor in the decline in marriage after the

Famine. In fact, the Famine and post-Famine emigration was a catalyst of change in social attitudes towards the role of women in Irish life, which now became 'subject, subsidiary and restricted'. Some people worried about the lack of work for the increasing number of unmarried girls, particularly as 'the market for woman's labour was confined by tradition and labour within such limits that the supply is altogether superabundant'. Paradoxically, at a time of rising unemployment, a restrictive attitude to women's employment became current in the second half of the century: 'There was no need for a woman to work as long as she had someone to support her – a father, a husband or a son'. Few Irishwomen, however, could rely for their support on male family members.

The Census of 1871 mentions 273 annuitants in Galway. These were women who were legally entitled, under the terms of family settlements or as part of a bequest to an annual payment from family estates. However, documents reveal the difficulties encountered by some women in trying to obtain payments of annuities.

As women's earnings were not listed separately in official statistics, it is very easy to underestimate their contribution to the family. At that time, 'in the eyes of the law, whatever personal property belonged to the wife is absolutely vested in the husband'. As a consequence, all family income was listed as the husband's, even if he did not earn it. Even when women lived by begging (a form of 'work' adopted as a subsistence strategy by indigent females), they made a substantial contribution to family income.

Women jealously guarded any control over money traditionally theirs within the family. In some districts, such as the Claddagh in Galway, women managed all the family finances, including the men's earnings. In 1824, Dutton recounts that an instance occurred of a Claddagh man who wished to keep his own money but his wife's indignant companions threatened to burn his house and 'actually proceeded to speak such violence that he was forced to succumb'. After the Famine, women's contribution to the household was more in terms of labour, unpaid and undervalued, than money. Several authors pointed to deficiencies in the educational system and blamed 'want of education' for female unemployment; they needed 'a sounder knowledge of the elements of arithmetic and book-keeping'. Such a lack was not confined to the very poor. The daughters of gentlemen should be given 'a moderate special education and an industrial turn given to their minds'. Such an education was seen as a permanent security against distress.

However, for many women in Ireland, 'all was changed, changed utterly', particularly after the Famine, which exacerbated trends already in evidence in the earlier part of the century; and for many women a loss of status directly related to unemployment with a consequent decline in marriage prospects, with few chances of improvement except by emigration or obtaining one of the few jobs available. Much of the loss of status was gender related and there is more than a germ of truth in the statement that 'daughters were largely redundant in nineteenth-century Ireland'.

For women who remained in Ireland, many factors operated to push women out of employment as the century progressed. Joanna Bourke (1993) asserts that in communities experiencing a contraction of employment, women were impelled to maximise their possible economic contribution by focusing their energies on domestic work for the family. This occurred at a time when there was more housework to do, as people moved into larger houses; improving living standards stimulated housework, which in turn raised living standards. The collapse of certain employment sectors traditionally reserved for women stimulated a shift of female labour into the home, which, in turn, encouraged the further substitution of men for women in the employment market. The coincidence of sectoral shifts in the employment market, investment in the rural economy and capital requirements of the household was crucial (Bourke: 1993: 264). It is quite possible that women resented this development, yet in the circumstances of the time, it seemed to many that it was the best way to minimize the risk of poverty, in the absence of other waged employment opportunities.

HOUSING

For much of the century, bad housing was the norm in Ireland.
Dutton, writing in 1824, described conditions within the unhealthy,
crowded cabins of Galway, which frequently consisted of one room:

> There is scarcely a cottage that has not a step down into it
> and a dung-hill uniformly near the door. To the bad effects
> of a damp situation may be added the want of ventilation,
> which in general is confined to that between doors; for if
> there is a hole in the wall with a pane of glass fixed in it, it
> is the most they possess; as to the window that opens, that
> is a luxury possessed by very few except show cottages. In
> too many places, the cow and pig keep their places in the
> house; certainly not so frequently as formerly.

Gustave de Beaumont, the noted French traveller, writing in
1839 noted the poor building materials and widespread lack of
chimneys. He described the pig as:

> the only thriving inhabitant in the place ... The presence of
> the pig in an Irish hovel may at first seem an indicator of
> misery; on the contrary, it is a sign of comparative comfort
> ... Indigence is still more extreme in the hovel where no pig
> is to be found.

Poor people in the country and in most towns, except
Ballinasloe, Headford, Mountbellew and Woodlawn which had
progressive landlords, lived in terrible conditions. Cottages were
small; in Kilconnell, for instance, they ranged from 18' to 21' in
length and were about 13' wide, with walls varying from 6' to 8'
in height. In Bohermore, in Galway City, there were about 1,000
miserable hovels. Housing in the city was falling into decay
because of the decline in trade and commerce caused by the
depression of the 1820s. This trend continued, as Carlyle in 1849
described the city as one long row of huts, mostly or all thatched.
Cabins were usually built on poor sites, along the verges of roads

and bogs, on the least valuable land as people feared wasting any land that might be productive.

Generally, the cheapest local building materials were used. Stone was widely used for loose stone or dry stone walls, in parts of Ballinakill and Omey. Some cabins were built without mortar, as in Tuam and Beagh. When mortar was used, many materials such as clay and lime were used. Most cabins, however, were not plastered inside. Exceptions were Kilcummin and the Aran Islands, where internal walls were plastered with mortar of lime and sand. Chimneys, once rare, were becoming more common in the 1830s, but some consisted merely of wickerwork, coated with mud, as at Ballinakill and Clonrush. In many cabins, the smoke went out either through the door or a hole in the thatch. Windows were generally found in towns, more rarely in the country; at times, the window spaces had no glass. A great variety of roofing materials was used, such as straw in Killanin and in Loughrea town, sedge or straw in Omey and Ballinakill, sods in Killimor and Tiernascragh. Some cabins had no door. Women lived more comfortably in some areas, such as Aran, where cabins, built of stone had a central chimney and were plastered on the inside – in stark contrast with the mud cabins in Killoran and the rural district of Loughrea. From parish to parish cabins varied widely. In Killimor, Tiernascragh and Clonfert, the cabins were built of bog earth, clay (dóib), or dry stone walls, according to their respective localities.

The workmanship in the cabins was poor; indeed, many cabins could be called *teach gobáin* or jerry-built by *gobáin* or incompetent tradesmen. In Clonfert, those built of loose stones were 'plastered slovenly'; in Connemara, they were badly thatched. Clay floors were damp for much of the year due to the bad roofing. Necessary repairs were badly done; when it rained, repairs were sometimes carried out using potato stalks and thistles.

Even when people were a bit better off, the cabins generally remained bad and dirty except in coastal areas, where there was good fishing almost up to the Famine, when herring stocks became scarce. Housing in Claddagh is of great interest. In 1808, Captain Hardis, who noted that every little cabin was 'stored with the

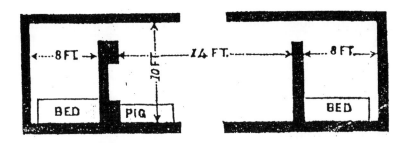

6: Plan of a prosperous cabin in the Aran Islands

7: Connemara cabin (1843) with 'original Connaught pig' (Hall)

whitest delft' had organised a scheme among the fishermen there, whereby they paid a small sum weekly for paving and cleaning about their houses, which eliminated many of the prevalent diseases. Later, Hardiman (1820) attributed the cleanliness of the Claddagh cabins to the fact that they did not contain any cows. Conditions within cabins in other parts of the county were very poor. Inglis, in 1834, described one such cottage as being deficient in almost every article of comfort. He also noted that the prosperity of better-off households was not reflected in their accommodation. Such miserable conditions were described by the Devon Commission (1844) which mentioned, for example, Tully, whose cabins typified the housing built by peasants on road or mountainside:

> If by the roadside, instead of raising his dwelling above its level so as to secure it from the damp, he invariably sinks it below, considerably below the level of the highway, making it in fact a drain to the road.

Sir William Wilde (1852:91–2) described his friend Paddy Walshe's cabin shortly before the Famine, giving details of many common superstitions and arrangements:

> Upon the hip of the roof, to the right of the doorway, grew a luxuriant plant of house leek to preserve the house from fire and the inmates from sore eyes. Upon the threshold was nailed an ass's shoe, to keep off the fairies and preserve the milk; and on the lintel was cut a double triangle, like what the freemasons have adopted for one of their mystic signs in order to guard the children from the evil eye …
>
> The ROOM, which was separated by the chimney and a low partition from the rest of the house was all in darkness.

In Kilmacdaugh and Kilbecanty, there were many one, two or sometimes three apartment cabins. In most areas, however, the fireplace was in the centre of a one-room cabin, and formed the cabin's focal point. Women's attempts to ensure acceptable living conditions were hampered by the small-sized cabins, damp floors, dark interiors and the presence of pigs and fowl, which were invariably kept indoors as it was believed that 'smoke and warmth was beneficial to them'. Hens received particular attention when eggs were hatching. Eggs, were now sold to pay rent or buy clothes. Young goslings were also kept in, to ensure good quality geese for the Christmas markets, a major source of income and to prevent them from being stolen. Goose eggs were used by the families. Animals, such as cows, frequently shared cabins because of the absence of a pig-sty or back-yard.

Cabins were disease-infested. The poor food and living conditions, lack of clothing and poor water supplies all contributed to the spread of disease. With polluted water came typhus, 'an unerring index of destitution'; lack of good water was noted even in larger towns and Galway City. Urban overcrowding helped to spread disease. As conditions declined in the countryside, many of the rural poor began to drift into the towns, where they found only poor, squalid accommodation as the effects of disease and the decline of small-scale industry, hit by mechanisation, caused the stagnation in Irish towns in the first half of the century. For a time, however, during the cholera epidemic of the 1830s, the wealthy fled from the towns to the countryside to escape the contagion in the towns. In the countryside, however, the proximity of dung-heaps helped the spread of endemic insect and fly-borne diseases. It was very difficult, in such conditions, to ensure the health of babies and young children. Long before the Famine of the 1840s, women lived in dread of illnesses, particularly those which occurred in summer, including fever to which young people between the ages of 16 and 20 were particularly susceptible. Women between the ages of 35 and 50 often fell victim to fever. Smallpox and measles were the major killers of young children. Mothers frequently died of puerperal fever, caused by the unhealthy living conditions.

The congested cabins, many of which lacked bedsteads and even bedclothes, were totally unsuited to nursing the sick. Fever

8: An Aran Islands scene

inspired such a fear of contagion, that women who could rely on the help of their neighbours in almost any circumstance, could not count on it at such a time. Sometimes, even family members stayed away, particularly if it was suspected that a sick person had contracted the 'wasting disease', possibly consumption, which killed many people between the ages of 26 and 50.

Not all housing in the county was inferior, however. Many country houses had been built in the county during the latter half of the eighteenth century, including Coole in Gort, Tyrone House in Clarenbridge and St Cleran's in Craughwell. In the early decades of the century, many new country houses were built, including Lough Cutra Castle in Gort, Garbally in Ballinasloe, Castlegar

9: An eviction in progress

in Ahascragh and Moyne Park in Monivea. Several landlords were compelled by penury to sell out after the Famine and some of the new owners lived in their great houses. Some smaller gentry lived in the county, in rather unostentatious houses, such as Danesfield; by contrast, the seats of the opulent gentry 'were numerous and well-built'. County Galway had 161 mansions, many of them built along the coast road in scenic areas; they were regarded as a good investment, because of the fishing and shooting rights which attached to them. By 1870, County Galway had a larger number of landlords than any other Irish county; about 400 landlords controlled all the productive land in the county, Lords Dunsandle, Berridge, Clanricarde and Clonbrock owning a total of 300,000 acres.

By a strange quirk of fate, the Great Famine, which brought such misery and tragedy, helped to improve the lot of women, as

10: The aftermath of eviction

11: A dispossessed family. Note the *duidin* or clay pipe,
widely used by women at that time

housing improved in its aftermath. There was a drastic decrease in the poorest form of housing, 30.4% in the rural districts and 10.1% in Galway City. This was the so-called 'Fourth-Class House,' an 'all-mud cabin having only one room'. These had been occupied mainly by members of the cottier class, who had been decimated by the Famine. Yet, there were still amost 10,000 of these cabins in the county in 1871, although most of them were now built of stone rather than mud. In the same year, 3% of the houses in the county could be classified as first-class and these included the houses of the gentry. By 1871, most people lived in third-class houses, which 'while still built of mud, varied from three to four rooms and a window'. This was a marked improvement. In the earlier part of the century, few landlords were interested in improving housing conditions for their tenants. Improving landlords were generally resident and solvent; among them were Lord Cloncarty and Lord Clonbrock who built fine tenants' houses, with iron window frames, good ventilation and lighting. In the last quarter of the century, there was much acrimony among farmers and farm labourers regarding the provision of labourers' cottages.

The interiors of many cabins and houses remained squalid and must have caused intolerable strain, if not mental illness, in many women. The greatest deprivation was possibly the complete lack of privacy, particularly in one-room cabins. Many women tried to eke out a living in their cabins, although hampered by darkness and possibly swirling smoke. There was no provision for suitable storage and containers of all kinds were treasured. Because it was almost impossible to keep clothes clean, great emphasis was placed on storing materials and bags above floor-level, safe from smoke and moths. Those better-off had chests to store blankets and clothing. Containers for food and smaller items were very important. Great stress was placed on keeping salt dry, as it was the only condiment or 'kitchen', which many people could afford and so it was stored near the fire. Baskets were a boon, because they could be made cheaply of local materials and were easily replaced. Baskets were also used to bring meals to those working in the fields and eggs to the market. Women often served food, such as bread and potatoes in baskets. Baskets used to serve potatoes were called *skibs*. Many women used the *cliabh* or back-basket to carry turf or sea-weed. The struggle to keep the interior of the cabins clean was unending. The quality of the bedding means that the cabins were lice-infested, causing itching, skin diseases and interrupted sleep. It was impossible to keep floors clean, where straw was used as bedding and animals were allowed to roam freely. Foul smells further polluted the cabins, wafted from dung-heaps which were inevitably sited near the front door. It has been argued that women could have done more to improve living conditions within the cabins. However, in areas such as Connemara, women undertook much of the labour in the fields and along the seashore. Connemara men of the time were castigated for leaving the heaviest burden of the work to their womenfolk, thus leaving them little time for housework.

Accounts in *Saunder's Newsletter*, for example, remind us that living conditions hardly changed over a long period. Generations of women lived their lives, without ever having known decent living conditions. In general, landlords did not make themselves responsible for maintenance of houses occupied by their tenantry. Many clusters or *clacháns* were built around communal wells; since some had cesspits, it is quite conceivable that seepage helped the spread of disease. Good spring wells were highly valued and many women earned their living as water carriers, even in towns. Cholera was endemic and the authorities were preoccupied with its prevention. Thus, Nuisance and Disease Prevention Acts had been passed in 1848 and 1849, which governed the disposal of dirt and waste material. The Sanitary Act of 1866 did much to improve the general quality of life for people as a new official appointed under the terms of the Act, the Sanitary Inspector, was charged with 'the maintenance of proper drainage, the supply of clean water to the populations of towns and villages, and the prevention of overcrowding in dwelling houses'.

A huge divide existed between the lives of women in the great houses and the cabins. In normal times the difficult lot of poor

12: Animals were also famine victims

women was alleviated by female camaraderie, probably reinforced by the rigid gender divisions prevalent in Ireland. Women were particularly fond of visiting, particularly on Sundays, which provided occasions for story-telling, spinning parties etc. Women who lived inland liked to visit the seaside in summer, and collect some *bia trá*, such as carrageen and dilisk (edible seaweeds). In winter, people stayed in as much as possible. Story-telling, song, knitting and spinning were popular pastimes then. Women did not suffer from isolation or loneliness in clustered settlements called '*clacháns*', such as Roo near Kinvara and between Galway City and Spiddal. Later, many felt isolated in dispersed settlements. Close proximity, however, caused many minor squabbles, such as disputes about trespassing, which were frequently tried by the petty sessions.

Homelessness became a major problem during the century. This generally occurred as a result of evictions at different times, such as those which took place for non-payment of rent. In such cases, people sometimes built temporary shelters called *scailpeens*. Landlords who bought estates under the Encumbered Estates Act frequently found large numbers of unauthorised tenants living in

[35]

such shelters. This, in turn, led to further evictions. Some women
became homeless with the break up of families during and after the
Famine, if they were unmarried mothers, old and unable to contribute to their households and lacking in family support. The
Gaelic phrase for homeless is '*gan teach, gan treabh*', that is, without
home, without family. For homeless women, in very many
instances, the workhouses became refuges and sanctuaries.

In retrospect, one can only pity the poor women, who spent
their lives never knowing decent living conditions, never perhaps
having a regular supply of food or a proper change of clothes in
their continual struggle against grinding poverty.

CLOTHING

The poor quality of the clothing worn by Irish people was the
subject of much comment in the nineteenth century. Kohl, a
Germany traveller, said in the 1840s that 'the rags of Ireland were
quite as remarkable a phenomenon as the ruins, no such rags
were elsewhere to be seen'.

This description is particularly apt for the clothing of the
people in Galway during this period. Many people were confined
to their cabins in winter, through the want of ordinary clothes.
Indeed, many poorly-clad people remained years from their
places of worship.

Clothing that was available was made of poor quality, coarse,
low-priced materials, such as corduroy, cotton or frieze. Men
were generally better dressed than women or children, many of
whom were almost half-naked, particularly in summer. In the
poorly-ventilated cabins of Camus, people used the smoke from
the fire to keep children warm, as a substitute for clothing. At
times, people were forced to cut up blankets to make clothes. On
public occasions, such as holy days and fair days, men were rarely
without shoes and stockings; women were generally without
either, but the children always so. When women who had shoes
were travelling to town (such as the women from Barna selling
butter in the Galway market), they frequently carried them and

Connemara Women

13: Connemara women in a variety of dress (1880)

did not put them on until within walking distance of the town, in an effort to prevent wear and tear. Women in coastal areas were generally better clad than those inland, reflecting the comparative prosperity of the fishing industry for part of the century.

When they could afford it, women liked clothing of bright colours. Red petticoats were frequently worn, although some women in areas such as Omey wore cotton gowns on Sundays. In Claddagh, several women wore very expensive hard-wearing cloaks of creamy-coloured undyed material, while many less well-off women wore shawls, which were a mark of poverty. Ribbons were popular, except in Claddagh, where the women were described as being very expensive in lace for their caps. Most frieze and home-knitted stockings were made from home-produced wool. Changes in the price of wool, however, affected clothing badly. In 1836, the price of wool was twice as high as it had been in earlier years. There were also far fewer sheep in the country. For this reason, those who had wool found that it paid them better to sell it and purchase coarse cloth than to get it manufactured: 'It is not those who would manufacture for them-selves that have the sheep'. By the time of the Famine, many ordinary people could not afford to clothe themselves in woollen garments, because of the high price of wool for several years. Starvation forced many people to slaughter their sheep, thus leaving them without a supply of wool; this development also affected the supply of bedding adversely, as blankets had been woven on hand looms in the cabins. Clothing became progres-sively worse for most people during this period; many people, indeed, lacked a change of clothing, which affected appearance, health and school attendance and was a potent factor in spreading and prolonging illness. Some felt that cold from the want of good clothing caused more illness than contagious disease. Many could not afford new clothes or clean the old ones. Washing clothes, a task made more difficult by frequent unavailablilty of soap, was often carried out by 'beetling' performed by a woman standing up to her knees or higher in the water of a stream or river.

Migration also affected domestic weaving and spinning in a variety of ways. Because of poverty, there was a great demand for second-hand clothes, particularly woollen goods, often sold at fairs or markets. Enterprising migratory labourers in England and Scotland took advantage of this market to earn a profit. In Scotland, such labourers, called *troggers*, bartered Irish linen for old woollen clothes, which they sold or bartered in Ireland. Many people went to England to earn enough money to buy clothes for their children. They bought second-hand clothes overseas before they returned home after the harvest. As Galway had a high rate of migration, cottage industry was badly affected by these developments.

Clothes were frequently pawned, particularly from April to August and redeemed after the harvest. Many people pawned their best clothes before they entered the workhouses and redeemed them on leaving; they felt that the pawnbroker would keep their clothes safely. We will discuss the question of clothing

14: 'Tuirne Mhaire' (Mary's spinning wheel)

in workhouses in the chapter on the Great Famine and the provision of clothing to the needy outside workhouses in the chapter on the Relief of Distress.

Particular efforts were made by many organisations to provide clothes for poor children. These included the Presentation Sisters in Galway City, who took over the well-known Female Charity School and who were enabled to clothe many of their pupils with the help of charitable organisations. In February 1848, the Sisters received from the Society of Friends 40 garments, four pieces of grey calico (240 yards), 192 yards of blue calico and 92 yards of flannel. In March 1848, they also received £40 for clothing from Count Stereleski of the British Association. The Dominicans in Claddagh enabled poor girls to make their own clothing in their Piscatory School, one of three schools founded by the Dominicans in the Claddagh. While the main emphasis in this school was on vocational training for the fishing industry, domestic skills were taught to pupils as a survival strategy. In Esker, near Athenry, the Dominicans clothed 50 of their poor school pupils annually.

As well as many children, vagrants and the aged poor suffered from lack of clothing. Very many destitute old people were dependent on the support of their poor families. Many families, happy to feed old people, particularly family members, were loath, or indeed unable to clothe them; they found it difficult to clothe themselves. Old people felt, however, that good clothes added far more to the quality of their lives than food. Sometimes, people who lacked clothing resorted to begging and sold surplus food to buy clothes. Vagrants would not purchase good clothes, even if they could afford them, for that would destroy their trade. Dirty clothes and a filthy appearance were often assumed by professed beggars, especially in towns; to excite pity, some also brought ragged children suffering from afflictions, such as deafness, with them. Several women, perhaps unwilling to beg, stole clothes and, if caught, were tried either at the petty sessions or assizes.

It is not easy to quantify how much women and girls spent on clothing. The following figures show expenditure for three years by a labourer and his wife in the parish of Aughrim in 1836.

Husband	£	s.	d.
One hat	0	3	0
One frieze body coat	0	16	11
Three waistcoats, at 1s. 8d. per	0	5	0
Two pair of trousers, at 7s. 4d. per	0	14	8
Three pair of shoes, at 6s. per	0	18	0
Six pair of stockings, at 1s. per	0	6	0
Six shirts, at 2s. per	0	12	0
Total	3	15	7
Wife			
One cloak	0	9	6
One gown	0	6	0
One petticoat	0	2	8
Three shifts	0	3	9
Six caps	0	3	0
Three aprons	0	3	0
Two handkerchiefs	0	3	0
Total	1	10	11

15: 'Important business belongs to women'.
John Gregg, 28 February 1856

It is interesting to note that the woman spent no money on
shoes. Such a budget would be typical of many of the poor in the
County. On the other hand there was a sizeable minority of
women, including many who lived in the big houses of the
county, who provided much employment for dressmakers and
seamstresses and were well dressed. An advertisement in the
Galway Vindicator on 19 March 1847 shows the range of millinery
available to well-off fashion-conscious ladies, even during the
Famine. Stores such as Moons of Galway had been founded to
supply some of the fashion needs of well-off families.

Women felt very deeply about poor clothing and lack of
footwear, and when they emigrated, they rarely went barefoot;
they changed their habits with regard to dress more than in any
other respect. When they obtained regular work in Scotland, for
example, they soon purchased showy clothes. Those, however,
who had to enter workhouses overseas, such as that in Edinburgh,
were very indifferent about their clothing. The trend towards
better clothing was also noted in the United States.

For the poor, who remained in Ireland, clothing seemed to
improve very slowly. A visitor to Gort in 1862 spoke of the 'old blue

cloaks on the women and greasy-looking rags on most of the men'. Styles and colours, which were popular in the earlier part of the century, continued to be so. After the Famine, people began to buy much of their clothing as the replacement of the older conacre system by cash wages accelerated the decline in weaving and spinning. With the exception of the linen industry in North-East Ireland, domestic industry in the rest of Ireland was adversely affected by the rise of mechanised textile manufacture in England and Scotland. This led to a decline in payment for domestic textile production when many cheap calicoes became available as competitors to the traditional woollen cloths domestically produced. While it was asserted that people had quite got out of the system of making their own clothing, it is of note that the needlework syllabus of the national schools included instruction in making and cutting out of simple garments as well as knitting and mending. This would suggest that the cash-starved poor still made many of their own clothes and mended them, when necessary.

The lives of the poor, whether sick or healthy, at home or in the workhouses, idle or working indoors or out-of-doors, were greatly affected by the standard of clothing they could procure for themselves. The poor clothing worn by many women also reflected their inferior position in Irish society. It was argued that:

> a woman in Ireland has a lower status than a man as may be inferred by her worse clothing and from her being the first to suffer privations. If a family's circumstances improved, women still lost out and it was observed in an improving district, shoes and stockings are first seen on the men.

While procuring sufficient clothing was a major concern for women for much of the century and was a subject of comment by commentators and visitors to Ireland, yet it was the provision of food and housing which were of far more moment to many women and their families, particularly in times of crisis.

FOOD

A poor middle-aged Irish woman in the years immediately before the Great Famine would have looked back nostalgically to the years before 1815. At that time, although rent levels were high, prices obtainable for agricultural products were also high and it was less difficult to provide food for one's family than in later years. People continued to grow potatoes because of their high yields; in many cases, the poor lived on potatoes only – the cheapest food in the country.

The paradox of Irish poverty was that economic hardship forced a large section of the population to subsist on a single foodstuff which was, fortunately, very nourishing. Oats provided subsistence food for people during periods such as the 'meal months' when potatoes were scarce. In the late 1830s, the meal months were not as severe in some districts as in earlier years, as the extensive cultivation of prolific varieties of potato (lumpers and whites) enabled supplies to be eked out for most of the year. Prices recorded at the Galway market in July between the years 1820 and 1843 reveal that the average price of potatoes ranged from 4d.–5d. per stone. Average prices conceal wide seasonal fluctuations, however; within the county, there were wide variations. Early potatoes were very expensive and people who could afford to do so used oatmeal during the scarce season. Poorer people continued to use old potatoes which in many years were still available in July as the potato crop matured approximately 3–4 weeks later in the west of Ireland than in the east of the country. Later sowing in the west suited the boggy ground on which much of the potato crop was planted. Old potatoes were less expensive than early potatoes or oatmeal, which was quite expensive during the summer months. The average price of oatmeal in the Galway market between 1825 and 1835 ranged between 11s. 8d. and 12s. per stone. Oatmeal was much dearer than maize for much of the century and therefore imported maize was used widely particularly in years of economic difficulty, long before the Famine. Its attraction as a substitute for the potato was its cheapness, as maize usually cost at least 2s. less per cwt. than oat-meal, a not inconsiderable price difference for those on limited incomes.

Wages paid had an effect on the type of food consumed. Wages of casual labour were subject to seasonal fluctuations, thus making it difficult in the extreme to work out real wages per hour on a yearly basis. There were also differences between the wages of skilled and unskilled labour in Irish towns and cities. Average weekly wage rates for the whole of Ireland were approximately 5s. 11d. in 1854, 7s. in 1868, 7s. 10d. in 1874. Wages to labourers were often paid in provisions and by conacre and in cash or some combination thereof. The basis on which provisions were valued has not been stated in official reports. However, it was felt that the payment of wages in the form of potatoes could lead to abuses, and there were demands for the abolition of the so-called 'truck system' of paying wages in kind to agricultural workers. However, during this period of rising prices, the value of payments in kind such as Scottish labourers received tended to rise, whereas the Irish labourer was caught in the scissors-like effect of nominal money wages, which were depressed by com-petititon for employment and rising rents for land as inflated produce price pushed upwards farmers' valuations of land let to labourers (Cullen, 1983).

Lord Clancarty paid his labourers in English currency, which was greatly valued, during the 1830s but was an exception. Bank failures in Ireland caused many people to distrust Irish currency in the earlier part of the century. Labourers were paid variously from £4. 10s. to £9 in 1836, for about 145 days' labour. Wages might be enhanced by some benefits, such as the use of two acres of land for tillage in the case of one herdsman. The provision of rations and apartments was frequently a part of the working contracts of head nurses, matrons and masters of workhouses. The matron appointed to the Galway Workhouse in 1843, received in addition to her salary of £10 per annum an apartment, coal, candles and a sufficient quantity of provisions used in the workhouse.

The fish market – Galway

16: 'Dúirt bean liom': trade and gossip at the Spanish Arch, Galway.
(Note subtle gradations of dress.)

However, when the Napoleonic Wars ended, there was a slump in the price of agricultural products; grain prices were the most depressed. Rents and the price of conacre were kept high because of population pressure which increased demand. Manured conacre cost about £5 per acre per annum in the 1830s. Along the coastal areas as Ballinakill (Connemara), all classes had reasonable food supplies up to 1815, but were poorly off by the 1830s, because of the fall in the price of kelp (their staple commodity), the failure of the herring industry and the price of cattle for export, which fell from £12–£13 per animal in 1815 to approximately £5 in the 1830s. However, people were worse afflicted in inland areas and many tenants let their rents 'run on them'; that is, they fell into arrears despite their best efforts. Many indeed, became insolvent, known locally as 'bad marks' while uncaring landlords or their agents continued to wring the highest rents (rack rents) from them. In order to survive and still pay rack-rents, people all over

Ireland became dependent on the 'lumper' potato, a high-yielding white potato, prone to disease. In earlier years, a less prolific variety of potato called 'cups' were greatly esteemed as 'they stay long in the stomach' but were generally much more expensive than lumpers. Also popular was cabbage, particularly a flat Dutch cabbage.

The provision of food was more difficult during particular periods, such as summer, particularly in July. Most women, irrespective of marital status or age, experienced difficulties at such times, difficulties which compelled many of them to beg. The dreadful monotony of the lives of the poor is particularly evident in the matter of food. Trevelyan (1849) truly noted that the Irish were living on the verge of human subsistence. The potato had become the staple item of diet and it has been estimated that a man, wife and three children would require 12–24 stones of potatoes per week, as they were eaten at every meal. They were sometimes eaten dry, without any 'kitchen' or condiment, not even fresh milk, which was often classed as a luxury, although buttermilk was sometimes served with them. This potato economy absorbed much unemployed labour: it supplied the food needs of 60% of the population and acted as a lynchpin within the wider agricultural sector.

The worsening economic circumstances after 1815 meant that not only people of the labouring classes but some ranks of craftsmen found it difficult to procure food; these included weavers and other textile workers, who were adversely affected by machine production in England and Scotland. Factors other than the fall in prices of agricultural products aggravated the dilemma – tithes, grand jury jobbing and the decline in the textile industry. There were a few places in the county where the conditions of the poor had improved, but the overall prospect was one of declining living conditions and increasing progressive malnutrition. It is worthy of note that the deaths which occurred during the several partial famines in the early nineteenth century were frequently due to bad diet and not starvation, which caused the malnourished to contract diseases, such as low typhus fevers.

[46]

Several medical officers deplored the dependence on the potato as a staple food. They felt that the lumper potato promoted disease, especially dysentery. Potatoes were deemed to cause illness, particularly if eaten in a par-boiled state, without milk, or if dug too early. Such unripe potatoes were pounded with salt and vegetables. Some doctors referred specifically to the link between malnutrition and disease and how wholesome food might be beneficially substituted for medicine in many cases; others, such as Dr George Heathcote in Oranmore, added variety to patients' diets by giving rice or oatmeal with some cordial or nourishing demulcent in preference to other medicine.

In truth, people were half-starving themselves to pay rent. Butter and eggs were often sold to pay the rent, or to procure tobacco, salt, soap and tea, even by people who owned a horse or two cows. Oats were grown for sale rather than domestic consumption, especially by labourers. While corn (wheat) was grown extensively, there was little available for the local population in years when the potato yield was low after the merchants and distilleries were supplied. Occasionally, salt herrings from Galway were sold in rural areas in winter and spring, when they were cheap. People in coastal areas such as Aran and Innisboffin had a better diet as both fish and potatoes were staple items there. Meat was rarely eaten, except at Christmas and Easter, when poor labourers bought pork at 2d. per pound or inferior beef. Some ate a goose or piece of bacon on special days. Summer was a nightmare season for food supplies. Lumper potatoes from the previous year's crop were regarded as unhealthy after Garlick Sunday (the first Sunday in August, which was the traditional date for digging and cooking the new potato crop). At this season, those who could substituted oatmeal for deteriorated potatoes, which were fed to the pigs. Most of the potato crop was not fit for use before 15 August or later. Renters of conacre generally laboured for others before sowing their own crop. In Galway and Mayo, the period which separated the end of the old potatoes and the coming of the new was marked by misery and starvation. Life became particularly difficult for women and children, forcing many of them to beg ('take to the bag') to obtain food. Men rarely begged in their home district; indeed, any man, whose wife begged was said never to experience hunger. July was called Hungry July, Iúil an Ghorta (July of the Famine) and staggering July. People also noted the greenish yellow complexion of those eating cabbage and other greens for survival. Even in an ordinary summer, food scarcities caused many people to welcome cabbage, without potatoes. Several people then ate *praiseach* (charlock) boiled with meal.

Who begged for food? The wives and children of migratory labourers (*cabóga*), migratory farm labourers (*spailpíní*) and unemployed labourers begged. Generally, people tried to beg at a distance from home. Many women travelled widely (even from Galway to Kilkenny) to maximise their return from begging. Others, the 'street beggars' however, went to nearby towns and villages. Thus, many women and children from the Loughrea area begged in the district of Kilcreest and people from Ballinakill came to Loughrea to beg. Many women felt the shame of having to beg and gave it up as soon as possible. Deserted wives, unmarried mothers and old women without families and, more rarely before the Famine, old women whose families had thrown them out, were forced to beg. Some old people had to depend on relatives other than their immediate families or neighbours for support. In places, such as Headford, it was felt that the aged poor got the best part from their neighbours, the worst from relatives. Daughters-in-law, in particular, were always grumbling and old people never had tobacco there. In very bad years, whole villages were supported by begging; in 1835, for instance, 150 families in the village of Kilcummin (Moycullen barony) were supported in this manner. In parts of Connemara, people set the potato crop and then begged at a distance from home. Wives of labourers who were 'in hold', that is in accumulated debt for rent or food, were forced to beg. These labourers were in a particularly difficult position as they were often compelled by necessity to work for 'under-wages', (reduced wage rates) whenever called upon particularly by middle-men to whom they were 'in hold'.

What kind of help did beggars receive? There were subtle gradations in the assistance given. In general, it consisted of potatoes at Christmas, or in the case of sickness, a little meal. At fairs and markets, a small coin was given by those in better circumstances. Beggars often received buttermilk; some received lodgings. In some cases, they begged 'a bed of straw' in one house and stayed the night in the next. The 'strange news' brought by beggars was valued although beggars were sometimes accused of causing dirt and carrying fever. Farmers always gave food to those begging, although the beggars would prefer to receive coin.

Many people chose to believe that the Irish people, especially rural dwellers, preferred potatoes to any other food, but there is ample evidence to show that this was not so. The general cultivation of potatoes and their almost universal use arose from their cheapness. Of special interest was the question of obtaining food supplies on credit or 'on time', which was prevalent in the scarce summer season. Some people dug out new potatoes when not the size of a pigeon's egg to avoid having to borrow. This practice had disastrous long-term results. Unfortunately, for poor people in particular, there was no way of preserving potatoes (except seed potatoes) from one year to the next; a bumper crop in one year did not lessen hardship the following year.

Those obliged to seek credit were exploited by gombeen men and scullogues. The gombeen (*gaimbín* = usury) man was described by Wilde as being 'among the country people what the bill broker and money lender were among the higher classes'. Senior Protestant and Catholic churchmen spoke of the poor obtaining both provisions and seed at rates of most unChristian usury, especially as prices for provisions obtained on credit greatly exceeded market prices, because the credit both in town and country was granted by scullogues (*scollóga*), farmers who had savings. They exploited the fact that there were few sources of credit available to the poor. However, the credit price of potatoes did not exceed the market price in the same proportion as that of meal, because potatoes are more perishable than meal.

The workings of the system are revealed by reference to the parish of Killimor. Here, those supplying provisions on credit always charged double the market price, frequently buying meal when it was cheap and giving it out 'on time', in times of scarcity. Some even refused to sell for ready money, anticipating super-normal profits in the scarce season. However, such practices did not always ensure exorbitant profits. In this parish, a local landlord, insisted on at least one occasion that some of his tenants who had given out meal 'on time' during his absence received little more than the market price. Other resident landlords issued meal on credit at market prices during periods of scarcity. Worst off, of course, were the tenants of some absentee landlords. In towns, such as Tuam, many of the poor resorted to pawnbrokers; in Galway City, however, there were some people with nothing to pawn. Landlords, such as James Burke of Loughrea, forbade trans-actions between his tenants and local usurers. He was horrified by 'the continual scene of pawning' in Galway.

In the Clifden, Ballinakill and Innisboffin area, an enterprising farmer, charged from 10% to 15% on money lent to buy fishing tackle, a common profit margin at the time. Some, such as the sick poor in parishes such as Moycullen, could not get provisions on credit; in other areas, the landlord granted relief to such people on the recommendations of the dispensary doctor. Many families accumulated debt over a number of years until they exhausted the sources of credit. Then, whole families were forced to beg. Men, who were ashamed to beg, ostensibly sought work with a hook in their hand or a spade on their shoulder. On occa-sions, they were given a meal. They sometimes continued in this manner from two to three weeks, while their wives and children begged. Traditionally, as men and boys got the best available food, one may imagine how badly some women and children suffered from malnutrition. Coastal dwellers had a wider variety of food, the so-called *bia trá* or *leas farraige*. During the late summer and early autumn, women and children who lived near heather hills or woods gathered whortleberries (*fraocháin*, fraughans), wild strawberries and raspberries.

The poverty of the period is reflected in the shortage of adequate cooking utensils. Vessels formerly repaired were discarded, as people could no longer afford to mend them. As a result, many now began to roast potatoes in the ashes (*gríosach*) by the fire. Left-over cooked potatoes were made into *fleatair*, flat potato cakes. When people slaughtered animals, much meat was wasted either through lack of skill or necessary equipment.

Once women obtained employment, they purchased furniture, clothes and above all, food other than potatoes. Similarly, labourers in steady employment, tried to buy a cow to supply both milk for the family and fertiliser to produce better crops. Few women and labourers, however, were fortunate to be in steady employment and the struggle to obtain food was, even before the Great Famine, grim and unrelenting. Women spent much time and labour transforming the potato crop into family meals. Of country women, in 1836, it was said that 'between weeding potatoes, digging potatoes, washing potatoes and boiling potatoes, they have hardly time to attend to anything else. They can never be clean and diligent in other matters until the nature of their food be changed'.

When Irish people emigrated, the quantity rather than the quality of their food improved when in receipt of good wages. The dress of women and children also improved dramatically. In Scotland, Mr Miller of Blantyre thought that the Irish improved their dress more than their food, because in dress they were liable to comparison with the natives, while in food and dwelling they were not. Food supplies were very slow to improve after the Famine and in 1861, the potato crop failed in Portumna, and hunger was rife in areas such as Errismore, south of Clifden, where two-thirds of the potato crop had failed. After the Famine, in 1849, Saunders noted that people were sowing turnips, cabbage and parsnips in an attempt to reduce dependence on the potato.

Food consumed by the people contrasted with the quality of the food they sold. In 1824, Dutton wrote lyrically of Galway dairy produce as follows:

The butter made at Barna is of a very superior quality ...
That to my taste is superior to any I have tasted elsewhere.
It is made of the natural colour of butter and not spoiled by
the addition of too much hot water which almost every
dairy maid uses to hasten the process.

After the Famine, those girls and women who remained in
Ireland often faced food shortages and near famine for very many
years. The death rate of young girls between the ages of 10–14
between 1881 and 1891, the main decade of land purchase, is
revealing. The female death rate was 140% of the male total at
that age, many of them dying of consumption, the common
name for tuberculosis during the period, a disease frequently
associated with malnutrition. It would seem that much of the
land of Ireland was purchased at the expense of the lives of its
young girls. One is inclined to think they would have agreed with
the comment passed on the labouring classes in 1836, which
stated that if they were transported, they would have good
clothing and enough to eat.

2

The Nature of Society

MARRIAGE

The marginal position of women in nineteenth century Ireland and the inability of a woman of any age to earn her own subsistence makes her more desirous to be married. Women require a husband to maintain them whilst young and children to maintain them while old. It is evident, therefore, that besides the usual motives for marriage, there are in Ireland many additional ones.

Ireland in the nineteenth century was known as a country which had a young population, mainly peasantry, very many of whom contracted youthful, improvident marriages. When contemporaries spoke of the 'peasantry', they referred to sections of the rural population, including the landless labourer and cottier, below the level of farmer. Landless labourers, ironically, had a freedom in contracting marriage unknown to those whose parents had some property, however little. Parents of landless labourers had no property to grant or withhold to enforce obedience in the matter of marriage.

In impoverished societies, such as pre-Famine Ireland, the prevalence of early marriages may be plausibly linked to the lack of parental control. Poverty meant that most people were forced to become economically independent at an early age, and that parents had little property or capital to pass on to them to enforce obedience.

In the 1820s, women generally married at 18–20; many of the males when they came of age at 21, and from then on to 30. These youthful marriages were still common in the 1830s, but by this time they were being called 'premature marriages', as a change towards later marriages or no marriage was becoming evident.

The very poor were often accused of being feckless and improvident in their attitude towards marriage: 'These classes do not consider how they may be able to maintain themselves and family afterwards'. This was a commonly held opinion, which was qualified somewhat by the statement of the Catholic archbishop of Tuam in 1834:

> Where there is neither house nor home, nor any provision for the two hands and two feet, they do not usually marry. They do not know any comforts, but it is not difficult in ordinary years to raise sufficient food for bare maintenance. Marriage is an indulgence and a temptation. No wonder they should yield to it. They cannot be called reckless, if by recklessness is meant utter indifference to all consequences.

A recurrent theme in interviews with the very poor was the difficulty in making provision for marriage. One witness to the Poverty Commission (1835) stated: 'What can a servant boy or girl lay by against marriage except the seed of a rood of potatoes'? Others were willing to marry, if they had the basic necessities of life:

> If I had a blanket to cover her, I would marry the woman I liked. If I should get potatoes enough to put into my children's mouths, I would be as happy and content as any man.

The incidence of early marriages was linked to the capacity of a small plot of ground to provide enough food, mainly potatoes, to feed a family. Parents, however, did little to hinder early marriages. In some cases they were relieved that 'someone else could do for their daughters'. At times, clergy were accused of promoting marriage, so that they might collect marriage dues. Others, such Bishop James Doyle of Kildare and Leighlin (JKL), were opposed to early marriages. He argued that 'poverty and population act reciprocally on each other, like cause and effect; remove the one, or lessen it, and you will thereby check the other'. There were gradations of poverty, even among the very poor. Even before the Famine it was observed that those slightly less distressed were least inclined to marry.

Parents of the very poor made what provision they could for their children. Some shared cabins with their married children; in Aran, there were at least 30 houses which contained two or more families. In Clonfert and Clontuskert, a 'spot of ground' and perhaps a cabin was provided for the young couple. Marriage for young people from families who held land was influenced by factors connected with the sub-division of land and the question of dowries. Young people in such families were more directly under the control of their parents who could cut them off from a share of the family property, however little.

It had been customary in Ireland to sub-divide land among the family. There was a predominant notion

> of the equal and inalienable right of all their children to the inheritance of their father's property, whether land or goods. This opinion, so just and reasonable in practice, is interwoven in such a manner in the constitutions of their minds, that it is next to impossible to eradicate it; in spite of every argument the smaller Irish occupiers continue to divide the farms among the children and these divide on till division is no longer practicable and in the course of two or three generations, the most thriving family must necessarily go to ruin.

Indeed, the custom was widely regarded as a major contributor to Ireland's disaster. Prior to the Famine, there is some evidence of 'impartible inheritance' (which occurs when only one child inherits the holding and there is no sub-division) among large landowners. The Great Famine accelerated the switch to this form of inheritance. On a practical level, under the new system, the ownership was passed primarily from father to son, either by primogeniture, where the eldest son inherited, or ultimogeniture when the youngest son inherited. This change had a profound effect on the lives of women, making marriage 'the female equivalent to the male inheritance of his parents' estate'. The question of the 'dowry' or more commonly called 'fortune' became increasingly important, particularly after the Famine, when women's economic status worsened, adversely affecting their prospects. 'Because the daughter had little to bring except the dowry she got from her father, her marriage prospects now depended more completely on him and she had to become more subservient to his wishes'. The dowry (Gaelic word *spré*) was an integral part of the match-making system of arranged marriages and may be regarded 'as the cost of entry for the farmer's daughter to another holding similar to her father's in size'. Indeed, one function of the dowry was to iron out differences in economic status, and it was the subject of much hard-headed bargaining. Inglis noted in 1834 that 'marriage in this country is a very commercial concern arranged by parents and respecting which there is as much higgling as about any other bargain'. Dowries were also important in towns as well as in the country.

What constituted a dowry? In Claddagh, the parents, if in good circumstances, combined to supply the price of a boat (or at least a share in one) for the husband, and this with a few articles of furniture commonly constituted the entire sum of the worldly possessions of the young couple. A cabin was sometimes provided for the married pair. In rural areas, among small farmers and labourers, the dowry might consist of a bed and bedspread; in other cases, it might be a 'spot of ground' to build a cabin. In the years after the Famine, parents were reluctant to pay one fortune far in advance of receiving another (from a son's wife) and encouraged their daughters to remain in service either at home or as hired workers. Much of the preoccupation with dowries was the result of fear, and reflected the vicious rivalries within the ranks of the rural poor.

Non-payment of dowries was a matter of litigation. People who married in church sought redress from the civil courts, (to enforce payment) not always successfully; most people did in fact marry in church, though in this century marriage was the subject of much statutory regulation by civil law. Catholic marriages were regulated by common law only, according to which, marriage depended on the consent of the partners and was lawful, if contracted before a validly ordained Catholic priest. The civil law did not recognise Catholic canon or church law, which forbade solemnisation of marriage before a minister of any religion other than a Catholic priest or before a civil registrar. On a practical level, the law of the land laid down that a religious marriage should take place in church in the morning hours. This was alien to the established Irish custom of having marriage celebrated at home in the afternoons. Because of a reluctance to register marriages with the civil registrar, many marriages were not recorded, because the Irish Act of 1845 did not contain the proviso (included in the English legislation of 1836), that a civil registrar should be present at all marriages. Marriages of Protestants were normally solemnised in church. Mixed marriages, of people of different faiths, presented many problems, requiring dispensations from the church authorities if one of the parties was a Catholic. When a Catholic bishop granted a dispensation, the parties first proceeded to the Protestant church to make their vows or, after 1845, to the civil registrar. They then went to a Catholic priest to renew their consent. A mixed marriage celebrated before a Catholic priest only was invalid prior to the Marriage Causes and Marriage Law (Ireland) Amendment Act of 1870.

Weddings were a major cause of celebration. Among the very poor, it was customary to use wheaten bread only on such occasions. Neighbours rallied around to ensure a joyous occasion. The question of dues caused some difficulty to Catholics; marriages dues were a major source of income to the priests, but a cause of hardship to their parishioners; some parishes had a sliding scale for weddings. Couples sometimes lived together unmarried 'for want of the priest's fee'. At times, marriage fees were paid by instalment. There was a strange form of snobbery in evidence with regard to payments to clerics: one was regarded as well-off and thence to be respected, if one could afford to pay for a dispensation from the banns, which were read prior to marriage. It was observed that

> The custom of seeking a dispensation from the publication of the banns was widespread, apparently because it was widely accepted that to have them published indicated disgraceful poverty or an inability to pay the fee for the dispensation.

Banns were not read from the altar, where a dispensation was granted. Also related to marriages was the question of 'de statu' letters, stating that an individual was free to marry and was not a possible bigamist. In the Registers of all denominations, these were supplied exclusively to men, generally at a cost of £1. This would seem to suggest that men had a greater propensity to contract bigamous marriages than women.

Non-marriage or postponed marriage became more common as the century progressed. The decline in marriage rates already apparent in the 1831 Census became more pronounced during and after the Famine assisted by the change in social classes during the Famine. In fact, 'a disproportionate number of Famine survivors belonged to classes with above average at marriage'. The continued population decline after the Famine years 'resulted from the widespread postponement of marriage, a peasantry determined to eschew its pre-famine practice of recklessly subdividing holdings to accommodate married sons or daughters'. Marriages in the years immediately after the Great Famine were fewer, both in town and country, as the prevailing despondency seemed to permeate all aspects of life, including attitudes to marriage.

There was an increase in the numbers of unmarried men both in the urban and rural districts, greater than the number of unmarried women; the impact of emigration is to be seen in the tendency of young, unmarried girls to emigrate. There was a large increase in the number of widows in the county between

17: 'Sunday best' clothes at Eyre Square, Galway

1841 and 1851 (7.12%). Figures for Ireland in 1881 bear a striking resemblance to earlier statistics in some respects. The ratio between widows and widowers remained constant (3:1), compared with 1851.

Widows derived some economic power from their position as head of the household. In a male-dominated society, legal status depended largely on finance; thus, poor, single girls were in a very invidious position. This is shown by the fact that unmarried women inmates were in a majority among able-bodied females in the workhouses. As late as 1881, 72% of the female unmarried inmates of workhouses in Ireland were aged between 15 and 50. There was great pressure on girls to marry:

> It is a terrible incident of our social existence that the resources for gaining a livelihood left open to women are so few. Openings to destitute women may be resolved into marry – stitch – die or do worse.

By contrast, marriage conferred full status on both men and women. A married woman of 20 had a more important position in life than a spinster of 50 and marriage meant a setttled life and a degree of independence unknown outside of it. It was the Irish tradition that the wife had complete control of the dwelling house and the fowl. A married women, however young, had authority in the home over her unmarried sister, unmarried sister-in-law and children. Marriage was regarded as a resource against the troubles of life: 'It is a blessing, if it please God, to find a shelter from every wave'. Children were generally regarded as a blessing. However, infanticide and abandonment were used to dispose of unwanted children. Girls sometimes used pre-marital pregnancy as a means of obtaining a husband. This, of course, led to loveless marriages; so also did many of the arranged marriages, particularly as the age gap widened between husbands and wives. There were many strains on marriages, such as poverty and cramped housing conditions.

The death of affection was noted by Poor Law officers during the Famine: spouses deserted both each other and their children.

Irish society was divided along gender lines and this led on occasions to 'the less affection that exists between man and wife among the country people in Ireland than is found to adorn domestic life in the humbler spheres on the other side of the water'.

Yet, in spite of all difficulties, marriage was the desired state. The notion that a girl could find real happiness outside of marriage does not seem to have been entertained, and unmarried ladies of uncertain age and prospects were objects of both pity and derision. Yet, they were not as badly off as the unmarried mothers, whose chances of marriage were almost certainly blighted and who generally were the object of public scorn.

UNMARRIED MOTHERS

Among the very poor, the lot of the unmarried mother was the most difficult. Accurate figures for the incidence of illegitimacy are not available before the second half of the century as civil registration of births was not introduced until 1864. To complicate matters, illegitimacy is rarely mentioned in parish registers. We have, however, a body of evidence on the lives of those unfortunate women. The general attitude of society towards them was that of scorn and derision, unless repaired by a later marriage. No such stigma, however, attached to the unmarried father. Yet, despite a general air of disapproval of these women, there were wide variations in attitude within the county.

In general, the marriage prospects of these girls were blighted. However, a more immediate difficulty which many unmarried mothers faced was how to obtain maintenance and child support. In truth, there was no law which compelled a father to provide for his illegitimate child. There were, however, three legal processes, used by sympathetic magistrates to enforce the father's contribution to child maintenance:

1 awarding damages for seduction;

2 enforcing a promise to help with the child's maintenance, said by the girl to have been voluntarily made by the man;

3 awarding damages against the man for impairing the girl's earning power by making her pregnant.

The second option was the most common, with the girl herself instituting proceedings. In some areas, errant fathers were 'generally worried into compliance'. In such cases, the father had the right of choosing between taking the child himself or paying for its support, or some alternative was generally worked out, when the 'child was reared' at the age of two or three. The mother was granted maintenance (called 'wages' in official documents) until the child was three years old. The mother was granted this, not as mother, but as nurse. The question of payments to unmarried mothers was a legal minefield. They were not granted until after the birth of the child, and had to be applied for within three months of the birth, unless there were special circumstances. From the 1820s, barristers had begun to question the judgements of the justices at the petty sessions, thus making relief slow and insecure. Formerly, in the absence of other proof, the mother's testimony was sufficient to secure payment. By 1835, however, the girl was required to prove some agreement, either direct or implied, on the part of the reputed father, and he was permitted to disprove her evidence by any method he could. An agreement could consist of a promise to provide medical help at the birth or to provide food, when the girl was expecting the baby. In judgements, dating from 1835, other circumstances were required, such as evidence of intimacy, company-keeping, flirtation or the like; but under any circumstance, a defence was admissible. Justices also became doubtful of their power to force maintenance payments, although previously it was considered that, like any other debt, it might be paid by distraint, that is seizing and selling goods belonging to the father, like any other debt; this presupposed that the purported father had goods or assets which could be sold. Some districts, such as Killimor, had no claims for such payments; others had few.

Many of the girls realised that the benefit of a maintenance order was frequently more apparent than real. This may account for the low number of applications made. Some magistrates were distinctly unsympathetic to such applications and some girls may have reached the conclusion that such an application was worthless. With regard to the reputed fathers, the possibility or reality of a maintenance order was often a strong motive to emigrate or abscond. If they stayed at home, the existence of a maintenance order carried little force in law, if they were unwilling to pay 'wages' to the mother.

An unmarried mother could attain respectability, if the father of her offspring married her, in which case the child or children were legitimised. Some men married the girls involved 'through dread of the Order' to pay maintenance. One may cynically surmise about the amount of support given in such cases to the women and children. In Moycullen, 12 out of 14 married the women in question. Pressure was frequently brought to bear on men by the clergy and magistrates to marry in these circumstances.

Illegitimate parents, or the parents of illegitimate children, rarely married, unless they were of the same rank in society. In Killimor, between 1832 and 1835, six illegitimate children were born. In three cases out of the six, marriage followed; in the other cases, it was morally impossible as two of the women were idiots and in the third case, the father was a married man. Some married lest the female's character should suffer 'from malicious reports'; it would seem that the reputation of the erring girls would continue to be a matter of vicious gossip, if they did not marry; if they did, however, it would seem that respectability was restored and her earlier behaviour (pre-marital sex and a baby outside marriage) forgotten.

In a few areas there was a tradition of support by men for their illegitimate children. Among them was Kilconnell, which had 45 such children, almost all of whom were supported by their reputed fathers. In Killalaghton, where there not more than 30 illegitimate children in a population of 600 or 700 families, about five were not supported by their fathers; their mothers supported them either by begging or going into service. In most areas of the county, such as Ross, lack of support was almost universal.

The most distressing cases were the mothers who failed to obtain support either from the child's father or her family. Several were forced to beg, while a small minority sank into prostitution. It would seem that the traditional kindness of the Irish to women with small children did not extend to the unmarried mother – if two women were begging, one having legitimate children, and the other illegitimate children, the woman with the legitimate children, if known, would be pitied more than the other. A few felt compelled to desert their children; others left their children with very poor people and were called 'unnatural'. Poor people hoped for payment in such cases, in order to pay their own debts. There was little official assistance for deprived, disadvantaged children. According to Acts passed in 1772 and 1774, vestries (meetings of the ratepayers of a parish to deal with parochial business) were to be held in each parish once a year at which over-seers were to be appointed with the duty of raising funds looking after the maintenance and education of children deserted locally. A sum of £5 was to be raised in respect of each child by a 'cess' (a local rate) shared equally by all parishioners. In the event of any parish refusing to raise the necessary amount, the judge of the assize could order the sum should be raised as he saw fit. (That such local taxes were deeply resented is to be seen in the male-diction 'Bad cess to you' still heard in rural areas in Ireland and among people of Irish descent in Australia and the United States.) Some children in Monivea were supported by the local Vestry Cess, others by the Catholic faithful. In the parish of St Nicholas (Galway City), deserted children were tended by neighbours 'from mere feelings of charity'. If a deserting mother were located, she would be forced to support her child; some who were unable to do so committed infanticide.

Unmarried mothers came from all ranks of society, but some girls were more vulnerable than others. Among them were beggar girls who hired themselves out to farmers and were the target of sexual advances by some employers or male members of their households; when some of them had illegitimate children, they were forced into beggary again. In Killimor, however, when

30–acre men had bastards by their servants, which occurred frequently, they reared the child and sometimes paid child support to the mother. Most unusually, the child frequently got a dividend of the property on the death of the father.

Foreign visitors frequently referred to the chastity of Irish girls. In 1836, for example, reference was made to the great domestic morality in Claddagh, where there were only two cases of bastardy in eight years. One wonders at the low rates of illegitimate births. The influence of religion, the harsh attitude of society, young marriages and arranged marriages exerted a powerful pressure on young girls. Legal considerations reinforced the prevailing social and economic norms, as there was no Bastardy Law and, until 1838, no Poor Law which might lessen the hardship of the unmarried mothers. This virtue was especially remarkable when one considers the almost total neglect of their education. Segregation of the sexes was strictly enforced, particularly in close-knit communities in a society, where, in different ways, both the culture of the community and that of the legal structure above it separated women from any formal economic or political economy.

Many girls found themselves pregnant with a promise to marry. Often the men were of a higher rank in society; such men were also blamed for the incidence of prostitution. Attitudes towards illegitimate children and their mothers varied widely throughout the county, and at times revealed a surprising degree of materialism and snobbery. In Omey Island it was stated that a woman who had a child by a poor man would be scorned, but one who had a child by a gentlemen would be looked up to on account of the money. In Headford, 'the amount of money determined everything', that is the public attitude to the woman.

Women of the lower orders, who had affairs with the gentry, sometimes married men of their own rank in society. In Ballynahinch a young man married a gentleman's Miss for which he received £100. When unmarried mothers were poor and dependent on maintenance payments, the sum of money was generally too small to overcome the objection to their unmarried status. What was the reaction to the children themselves? They were sometimes taunted. When they grew up they encountered frequent difficulties, especially when they wished to marry. A small farmer would object strongly to giving a daughter to an illegitimate son, unless he was quite well off. An exception might be made if the man was in all other respects eligible, especially if his reputed father had the rank of gentleman.

Some girls, desperate to marry, wittingly allowed themselves to become pregnant. They then accused the man involved of rape. Convictions for rape carried the death penalty and, if commuted, carried long terms of imprisonment or transportation. The charge of rape was often dropped, on the marriage of the parties involved. For example, in the year 1835, there were three such cases in Moycullen, which came to trial and all of whom married 'out of dock'. This was a fairly common pattern in towns and villages, though many men, realising that they might face such charges, absconded. Church authorities finally banned marriages which depended on the outcome of such cases.

This form of coercion can be understood when one considers that only married women attained full status in Irish society; many girls, seeing a particularly bleak life ahead of them as unmarried mothers, felt no compunction in resorting to such tactics to enforce marriage.

One group of unmarried mothers, who earned some grudging respect from their neighbours, were those who were kept by their paramours. In general, though, neighbours disapproved of unmarried mothers, though they were not completely excluded from society. Female illegitimate children do not seem to have been as harshly treated as males. This, ironically, may be a reflection of the poor status of women in society, as family good name, which passed on through the male line was deemed to be of great importance. There is a suggestion that unmarried mothers were condemned by women of their own social class, from whom one might reasonably have expected support. The general attitude was succinctly expressed in the statement that: 'Bastards will never make an equal match; their mothers are despised by their own equals'.

All deserted children were believed to be illegitimate. When children of a greater age than infancy (more than two or three years old) were deserted, the law made no provision for them and they generally became beggars, unless some kind neighbour intervened. Cases of desertion were notoriously difficult to prove. No evidence has been found of the practice of abortion, but there were some cases of infanticide. It is thought that bastard children were more frequently destroyed than was generally admitted; it was a crime rarely brought to light. There were many children buried in private burial grounds in the county, where there was no service performed, and no notice taken of them. It is possible that before the days of mandatory post-mortems after suspicious deaths, there was more infanticide than was generally suspected. Some witnesses to the Poverty Commission, anxious to present their districts in the best possible light, denied the existence of deserted children or the possibility of infanticide, or else attributed them to the neighbouring parishes. Lives of unmarried mothers became particularly difficult during the Great Famine, when both they and their children were excluded from the provisions of various relief Acts, thus adding to the awesome burdens of their lives.

WIDOWS

Unlike unmarried mothers, widows, most of whom lived lives of 'virtuous poverty', were highly esteemed by society. Very few of them were well provided for by their husbands, who, in general, were not in a position to do so. Labourers could not do so; as a result, many labourers' widows gave up their cabins on the death of their husbands and resorted to begging, as many of them had done when their husbands were unemployed. Many widows were rendered homeless by illness, as cabins were often demolished after death caused by such illness as cholera. Cholera seemed to kill young men, and in areas such as Aran, in which the disease raged for two successive years (1835 and 1836), had a large number of young widows. There was a parallel in the neighbouring county of Mayo in the same years, where Moygownagh had a similar high number.

Some towns, such as Oughterard, had many widows. This town had a population of 114 families, 22 of which were headed by widows, of whom only four were completely self-supporting. Some widows retained their lands, others did so for a time. The possession of a lease did not automatically guarantee security of tenure: a person might still be evicted for non-payment of rent. Sometimes sales were forced because of debt. Widows whose husbands were in joint leases often found that the other lessees insisted that they leave the tenancy, as they feared the widows would fall into arrears of rent, for which they would then be liable. Many widows were just unable to pay rent.

When widows were able to retain their holdings, there was great support forthcoming both from neighbours and from relations, who would be unable to undertake their whole support, though they might help by taking charge of one of the children. Tillage was often done for them free of charge and labourers very commonly worked for them on holidays and on Sundays. Some landlords were helpful towards widows. In Headford, Mr St George set apart about an acre ('widow's holding') on his estate for the widow's support, which he let to widows for a nominal rent or rent-free on occasions. This applied particularly if the widow had a young family. In the town of Headford, half of the widows held their houses rent-free, and at times received other help from the landlord's wife, Mrs St George. In Omey Island and Clifden it was the custom to grant a widow one or two years free of rent, or in particularly difficult circumstances, during her lifetime. Mr Blake in Ballinakill was also helpful. He stated: 'I have scarcely known an instance in which half an acre of land given gratuitously for a few years, has not enabled the poorest to bring up a family with the help of relations.' Absentee landlords, with rare exceptions, had little pity on the plight of widows.

Widows who had no families depended on the kindness of friends and neighbours; the widow with young children to support was in a particularly difficult situation. A few fortunate

18: 'Going to the market', Salmon Weir Bridge, Galway

19: 'Working woman walking along the canal'

ones had families who were kind to them; others had families who were as destitute as themselves and could afford them little practical help. Many widows carried the extra burden of supporting family members who were in poor health. Such a one was the Widow Lorkan in Killimor.

Fever often killed those in the prime of life, and thus one found several grandparents (usually grandmothers) caring for orphaned grandchildren, such as Mary Carr in Moycullen, and Widow Robins in Killimor. Some widows supported families who were a burden to them either because of bad behaviour or selfish conduct. Mrs D'Arcy, who lived in Killimor in a state of destitution worse than a common beggar, was one of these. Widows tried to support themselves by any work which they could do, rather than resort to begging. They did washing, knitting, sewing, peddled goods and acted as huxters, selling tobacco, apples, fish and other items. One, Widow Smith, who supported herself and two other family members, sometimes sold apples and onions. At other times she sold flour and meal; she got it by the stone on credit, and had to pay for one stone before she got the next. She did not sell more than two stone a week, with a profit of 2*d.* per stone. During the months of June and July she never ate a full meal. Enterprising widows were hampered by lack of cash. Some could not to afford to buy wool at 2*d.* a pound; had they been able, they could have made four pairs of stockings, which sold at 8*d.* a pair. A few widows kept public houses; far more sold poteen or illicit spirits. There was a general idea that 'poteen was much wholesomer than Parliament whiskey'. While one might be sent to prison for excise offences, convictions for such offences did not carry the social stigma attached to a prison sentence for such offences as theft. Though the profit on the sale of poteen was higher than on the sale of many other items, it was not high enough to encourage women to deal extensively in this commodity.

In towns some widows worked as water carriers, carrying water for shopkeepers. In rural areas some worked in the fields during the busy seasons of spring and autumn. Many of the widows who were skilled in spinning and weaving were badly

20: 'Offering for sale their beautiful Connemara stockings of every variety of hue and more especially red' (Thackeray)

affected by the decline in these industries. The demand for hand-made lace articles had also declined and with it the income of many town widows. It was generally believed that poor widows living in the country were 'positively worse off than those in the towns'. People felt that there were chances available to them in the towns, which were not available to many widows in the country; because of this, many widows moved to the towns in search of a better life, which often did not materialise. Some survived partly by begging and partly by industry. It was said that this combination of activities 'was half starvation' as many widows earned more by begging than by working. Some who were forced to beg felt the moral degradation so much that they begged far away from home. Others resorted to private begging in a very discreet fashion. One lady was described as being too genteel to be a common beggar. Women in certain areas resorted to a system of 'half-begging'. This was described as follows:

> They go privately and get a stone or two of potatoes from their neighbours and cover them discreetly with a little cloth; then, when the neighbours are tired of that, they buy

a few small fish, salt leaf and things of that kind, and they come to their neighbours when the people are at their meals, and bring their children with them, when they are always handed some of what is going; and they give a handful of salt leaves in return.

Those reduced to begging, either publicly or privately, lived in atrocious conditions. Very many widows must have been on the verge of starvation most of the time. Even those who retained their husband's land could seldom afford more than two meals per day. Generally, widows with young children had to beg to support them for at least part of the year. The fact that she had young children aided the widow to obtain charity but mitigated against her chances of obtaining employment. Prospective employers felt they would have to give a meal to the children, particularly if the widow was working for her food. Most prospective employers could not afford this.

There was little official help for widows; no petty sessions gave them assistance. In some areas there was a church Poor List from which they received aid. At times, they received a dividend at the church door with the other poor. Occasionally, special collections were taken up for widows, who were particularly destitute. In Galway City, the Revd Mark Finn, moved by the plight of some of the widows of his parish, founded the Widows and Orphans Asylum in 1824, a charity which supported 60 people. A group who were relatively prosperous some years before the Famine were the widows of fishermen. In the Killeries, they generally occupied the land held by their husbands; Mr Blake had always found these widows to be his best tenants. In Barna, the widows and children of fishermen who had not shares in the boats were supplied by their neighbours. Seven families had been supplied in this way prior to 1836, and families of disabled fishermen received some shares in the boats. However, the sea fisheries had collapsed along the Western seaboard before 1846 and widows of fishermen thus found themselves in dire straits. Their quality of life deteriorated far more than that of the ordinary labourer. Up to 1845, it had been remarked that, generally, the fishermen's families had better clothes and their houses were thatched and whitewashed. By 1847, widows in Claddagh were in the extreme of poverty. In the 1850s, herring nets were given free of charge to widows and poor fishermen during the harvest and winter seasons. The fishing industry had improved a little and thus these gestures were of some value.

Widows dreaded illness, particularly if they had young children in their care, or had nobody to care for them. If affected by illness, a collection might be made to help them, or a hut built for them to shelter them for the duration of the illness. This kindness was not always available, and thus in Black '47, the Widow Ford died without any of her neighbours to help her, because they thought she had fever: fear of contracting fever overcame the usual neighbourliness.

During the Famine, the workhouses became filled with widows and children, the aged and weak. They entered these Draconian institutions to fulfil the conditions to obtain relief, as set out by the Poor Law of 1838. After a time, it was decided that destitute women, with two or more legitimate children dependent on them, might be relieved in or out of the workhouses at the direction of the Guardians. This worked to the advantage of some widows.

During the Famine, many landlords used the infamous Gregory clause (whereby official assistance was unavailable to people who held more than a quarter-acre) as an excuse to clear their estates of tenants. In some instances, there may have been collusion between landlords and the Poor Law Guardians to enable the landlords to clear their estates. Needless to remark that many of the landlords were also Poor Law Guardians! One such case occurred in the Kilconnell electoral division. Dr Derry, Catholic bishop of Clonfert, complained bitterly about the mistreatment of a widow on 28 May 1848, as follows:

> I am aware of a widow Scannell, who at my insistence went to the bailiff of her landlord. He has since taken possession of her holding. She offered to him all the land beyond an

English rood and then sought relief, but was refused. I further directed her to make a solemn declaration to that effect before a Magistrate. She did so. Other widows, though, were allowed outdoor relief (without having to give up their holdings completely), but the Guardian only gave this woman the option of going into the Workhouse or bring her daughter into such a nursery of vice.

The bishop stated that the guardians sought to apply to her the more stringent rule in order to help the landlord force her to surrender her house and cabbage garden. Sadly, this was not an isolated case. By contrast, in Clifden, the Guardians were, by December 1846, prepared to give outdoor relief to those widows with two or more dependent children to keep the workhouse for able-bodied paupers.

Few widows remarried. If a widow had children and remarried, strong objections were often made by the family of the first husband, who feared that the sons might be disinherited. Very many widowers re-married. Thus, in Galway Civic District, widows (19%) outnumbered the widowers by 3 to 1. This may also be ascribed in some cases to longevity and also to the fact that women were some years younger than their husbands. Before the Great Famine, about 20% of husbands were 10 years older than their wives, but this gap widened considerably over time. Occasionally, widows became involved in prostitution as a 'consequence of poverty'. Archbishop John McHale was loath to admit the existence of prostitution in his archdiocese, especially among widows; yet, in 1851, there were 27 prostitutes and brothel-keepers in County Galway and four in Galway City. Of these, two were widows. In spite of all the vicissitudes suffered by widows of all ranks, they proved to be great survivors.

By 1851, there were more female than male heads of families with their children in 11 of the 18 baronies in County Galway. A large number had migrated, while others had emigrated. In contrast, male heads of households outnumbered female heads of households in every barony in the county in 1851. This may reflect a higher emigration rate among women allied to the fact that slightly over one-third of the widows of that county were in public institutions.

RELIGION

In the nineteenth century, most Irish people were Catholics. The Church of Ireland, commonly called the Protestant or Episcopalian Church, was a national or 'established' Church, but it accounted for only a small percentage of the population; smaller numbers of other religious faiths included Methodists and Presbyterians, who had also suffered under the penal laws. There were 25 Catholic churches in County Galway, 25 belonging to the Church of Ireland and a smaller number belonging to other denominations. In both the Roman Catholic Church and the Church of Ireland churches, there was an increase in the number of clergy, 20% in the case of the Roman Catholics and 29% in the case of the Church of Ireland between 1841 and 1851. In County Galway, the number of Scripture readers increased from 3 in 1841 to 49 in 1851, reflecting the work of the Evangelicals in the county in this period. Many curates were appointed to Catholic parishes, far more so than in the case of Church of Ireland parishes.

Much controversy arose from the payment of tithes to the Church of Ireland. Tithes, which were defined as a tax on the renewable produce of the land, were particularly resented by poor peasants, even though some crops, such as potatoes and flax, were exempt from the tax. Members of churches other than the Church of Ireland, had to support the clergy of two religious denominations. In time, the resentment which this imposition aroused led to the Tithe War, with violent episodes in which some women took an active part. Freedom from the burden of tithes was cited as an advantage of living in the USA. Both Catholics and Presbyterians were alienated from the Church of Ireland, Catholics permanently so because of religious perse-cution during the penal era. Catholic Emancipation was granted in 1829 but had little effect on most women's lives. There is little information available on certain aspects of religious practice, which was integral to the lives of many women. While people had a 'strong and living enthusiasm for religion' this is not reflected in the official figures for attendance at Mass for Catholics, first available in 1834. Attendance was low both in rural English speaking areas and even more so in rural Irish-speaking areas, which were more remote. Many people lived at a considerable distance from church; this was true, for example, of the old diocese of Kilmacduagh, which formed a largely rural Irish speaking area. Many people were not bound by church regulations to attend Mass; these included children, whose presence under the age of seven generally met with disapproval. However, when one takes into account the aged, nursing mothers and young children who did not attend Mass as they were not bound to, there was in fact a good attendance at Mass.

Priests visited the outlying parts of their parishes once or twice a year holding religious ceremonies in private houses. Such visits called 'Stations' served many functions. They afforded many people an opportunity of attending Mass and receiving the Sacraments. Several people confined their official religious practice to the Stations, however, and a Church Reform Programme designed by Cardinal Cullen sought to eliminate this custom. The Stations could impose financial burdens on poor parishioners, who felt obliged to provide luxuries for some priests, which they themselves rarely tasted. Not all priests were so demanding, however. The Church Reform Programme imposed hardship on women whose circumstances were such that they were unable to attend distant churches. Lack of suitable clothing, as well as distance, were given as reasons for non-attendance. Devotion to Our Lady, especially the Rosary, was important. Many shrines to Our Lady were objects of special devotion, called patterns (Irish, *patrún*). There were many patterns associated with saints such as Bridget, and holy wells. Several festivals combined religion with celebration. Organised Catholic ceremonial had almost disappeared as a result of the operation of the penal laws and this added to the importance of the traditional devotions in the lives of the people.

Pilgrims usually left at the shrines some token of their visit, coins or pieces of cloth.

The Irish Roman Catholic bishops in 1839 expressed their fears lest the superstitions and carnival atmosphere of many of the traditional festivities prevailed over their religious aspects. It was suggested that the priests were becoming more puritanical and condemned all the traditional practices except Lough Derg. However, traditional devotions continued, though in a muted fashion, in places such as Aran and Mám Éin, which was also noted for faction fights or *scrimmages* in which, however, the women took no part.

After devotion to Our Lady came devotion to St Brigid, in whose honour many wells were named. Several emblems such as the St Brigid's Cross made of rushes or the *Crios Bríde* (St Brigid's Girdle), were popular in different areas. Others used *Bratóg Bríde*, which was reputed to ward off various illnesses and the effects of the Evil Eye particularly feared in Aran. Many festivals were linked to the cycle of agriculture, St Brigid's Day marking the beginning of spring and *Lughnasa* (1 August) the beginning of the harvest. Of interest is Our Lady's Well at Kilnalahan. The traditional pilgrimage took place on Garlic or Garland Sunday, the last Sunday of July, when people also tried out the new potato crop. This festive pilgrimage was accompanied by crossroads dancing and the picking of *fraughans* or bilberries. On the same Sunday, much match-making took place at Tobairín Bhet at Clonkeen as well as traditional prayers. Some pilgrimages took place at the site of old monasteries, such as Abbeyknockmoy. Here, as elsewhere, the sacred and profane were closely linked. Beggars picked bilberries, known locally as *múineoga* and sold them to visitors. Because of the wide prevalence of eye ailments at the time, women collected water from Bran's Well in Duniry, reputed to be particularly efficacious in the treatment of eye diseases.

Great faith and great superstition co-existed. It was widely believed in parts of Connemara that ill-fortune would strike anyone selling wood for making coffins. Foreign visitors spoke of the credulous Irish who wore scapulars as a charm against danger and disease. At times, faith provided no protection against disasters, such as the accidental deaths in Galway pro-cathedral in 1842, when part of the choir collapsed during the Christmas ceremonies causing many deaths and injuries. Religion was particularly relevant at birth, marriage and death. Women were anxious to have their babies baptised shortly after birth because of the current belief in Limbo. Baptisms were only delayed in the case of mixed marriages, or where people did not have the required dues.

The question of priests' dues, sometimes called 'priests oats', was a grievance held by poor people who felt that their priests were becoming more prosperous. In Connacht people combined to resist the payments of priests' dues, unless according to a scale devised by themselves. Such opposition was part of the agenda of the Rightboy Movement, a secret oath-bound organisation involved in much rural unrest. However, members of some congregations, as in Moycullen, vied with each other to contribute dues on occasions such as weddings and funerals. By the 1840s, the 'pinching times' affected priests' dues, which in many cases, were now paid by instalment. Dues were expensive: in 1825, the dues for anointing were 2s. 6d., 3s. 4d. for churching and from a guinea to thirty shillings for marriage. The fee for Baptism was included in the fees for churching. Protestant clergy did not receive dues, although they did receive tithes, except in large towns.

What part did women play in church affairs? Very little, in fact, except in minor roles, such as being a witness at a wedding or sponsor at Baptism. This was true of all denominations. Unofficially, many women worked actively for charity. Becoming a nun was one of the few openings available to Catholic women to take an active role in the Church and gain a respected place in society. New orders of Sisters, such as the Mercy and Presentation, were directly under the control of the local bishop and were sometimes subjected to undue interference by domineering parish priests; yet they managed to retain a measure of autonomy, largely through the influence of their superiors, strong-minded women. In Galway City, both the Mercy Sisters and Presentation Sisters were victims of a parish priest who misappropriated some of their funds. Becoming a nun appealed to many young women. There were 48 nuns in the town of Galway in 1841 and 42 in 1851. Some succumbed to the Famine. There were no female religious listed for the other religious denominations. However, by 1851, there were six female sextons listed for Galway County (four male) and none for Galway City.

An examination of church registers reveals much of the attitude of society and the churches towards women. In the Church of Ireland parish register for Ballynahinch (Connemara), the mother's maiden name is rarely given in records of Baptism. In the list for dues received in the Catholic parish of St Nicholas South in Galway City, there is mention of 'Brown's daughter'; 'Widow'; 'Mr Sloper's child'; 'Widow Walsh'. Many Catholic registers listed the mother's maiden name in the case of Baptisms. An exception is the register for Ballinasloe, Creagh and Kilclooney for the years 1820–1: a Baptism entry for 2 February 1821, reads as follows: 'Elizabeth of Thomas Cosgrave and ——'. Such omissions were not confined to poor people. In the Church of Ireland register for Ardrahan, a record was made of the Baptism of Jane Taylor of James of Castle Taylor (of a very well-known family) and ——'. The mother's name has been omitted. In some registers, such as the Church of Ireland register for Ahascragh parish, the father's occupation is given. Similarly, in the case of churchings after Baptism, there seems to have been little effort made to identify the women as individuals. In the Catholic register for St Nicholas East in Galway City, there is mention of 'a Carman's Wife' and 'Mrs (Maid) Cruise'.

With the relaxation of the penal laws, religious communities started developing and openly resuming their traditional role of caring for the poor, the homeless and the sick. In the nineteenth century, at least 23 asylums, some operated by religious, were established to rescue and reclaim 'fallen women'. The title 'Magdalen Asylum' was given to many of them, including the one operated by the Sisters of Mercy in Forster Street, Galway. This asylum, engaged in needle and laundrywork, not only as a means of training the 'penitents' (as the inmates were to be called) but also as a means of financial support. The survival of these institutions depended on the goodwill and support of women in the wider community, and it was women in charge of households who kept them supplied with work. The *Connaught Journal* of 1 December 1825 noted that the Galway Magdalen Asylum was just one year in existence; there were six penitents in it on this date. In modern times, such institutions have been regarded as Draconian, yet they appeared as refuges to unfortunate females at the time, who were in many instances the outcasts of society.

Female religious played a great part in education, social work and famine relief throughout the period. The Mercy Sisters founded the Barna Soup Kitchen at the Quay in Barna. During the period 10–19 March 1847, 2,443 people were fed gratis. Efforts were chiefly made in areas of great social disadvantage, such as neglected girls. Ministers of religion, their wives and families gave assistance to the needy in a quiet unobtrusive manner.

Religious controversy, like an insidious poison, permeated the life of nineteenth century Ireland. One aspect of the controversy was the vexed question of proselytism which in its strict sense means attracting converts by the promise of material gain. A missionary movement, called the Second Reformation, was begun by the Church of Ireland, which hoped to gain converts through schools. Some Protestants, feeling threatened by the emergence of Irish Catholic political power after 1829, joined the Evangelical Movement, which was introduced into Ireland in the form of Bible Societies. While aiming to maintain a settled society, they nonetheless caused much religious strife. They offered free education to poor parents and were openly sectarian. Some of their societies, such as the Irish Society for Irish Church Missions and the West Connaught Church Endowment Society were founded during the Famine and were still in operation in 1868. Some members of the Protestant ascendancy, however, although unhappy about an 'unfettered' Catholic population, did not resort to the repressive methods of religious coercion associated with the Evangelicals. Following the change of ownership of estates following the Encumbered Estates Act, many estates were bought by Evangelicals, who generally ran well-ordered estates. Some

Evangelicals, such as the Revd A. R. Dallas, were very efficient. He founded his mission headquarters at Castlekirke on the banks of Lough Corrib, with the support of some local landlords. This was to be his headquarters for evangelizing Connemara. Four schools were opened for this purpose in Oughterard parish. Such schools had little chance of success in parishes which already had good schools. Proselytism was described as 'the bane of peace and social happiness in Ireland'. Galway had its share of acrimony and strife, even in remote Aran. Mrs Blake commented that Catholic priests did not attempt to convert members of other faiths but concentrated on protecting their own congregations. Death-bed conversions were suspected as having being caused by the undue influence of an over-eager clergyman and doctors were sometimes called to testify as to the behaviour of certain clergymen. Controversy raged from time to time, when attempts at proselytism commonly called 'souperism' were made in the Galway area by misguided zealots. Such attempts were roundly condemned by both the Catholic clergy and the ministers of the Church of Ireland. Happily, religious differences were put to one side in Galway city during the Famine. The Revd John D'Arcy, the vicar of St Nicholas' church, co-operated with clergy of all faiths to maximise famine relief for the city. Sadly, this peace did not last.

Over much of the county, attempts at conversion were linked to famine relief. People sometimes refused help from relief schemes which were linked to proselytism. Efforts at conversion were even brought into the workplace; several such attempts were made by the zealous but misguided Revd Mr Adair, of whom, it was said that 'his fanaticism haunts him like an evil genius'; his efforts inspired much hatred. Allegations of souperism continued after the Famine, often among the 'impoverished and uneducated inhabitants'; even though proselytisers maintained stoutly that they held out no pecuniary inducements. Many conversions were temporary, the converts sometimes returning to the fold, once economic circumstances began to improve. The behaviour of many Evangelicals outraged Protestant clergy such as the Revd S.G. Osborne (1850:242) who stated:

I cannot, however, but lament the strife, ill-feeling and but too often hypocrisy, which I fear is the result of the attempts made in this direction.

Catholic clergy in Galway did much to dampen the flames of religious controversy by ignoring the attacks of some of the zealots, although angered by the purported efforts made by proselytisers which were noted even in the workhouses.

Many Protestant clergy resented fanatical evangelicals, special interest groups, who crossed parochial and diocesan boundaries and were outside the control of the Established Church. The 'Second Reformation' allowed Established Church pastors to embark upon conversions, if they so wished, but they were, in general, more realistic than many evangelicals who held sanguine beliefs about the speed of conversion. The chances of making conversions was lessened by the fact that some evangelical clergy-men acted as land agents, often exhibiting blatant cruelty towards their tenants; such clergymen landlords aroused hatred and contempt for religion and may have a bearing on the fact that hopes of mass conversions were not fulfilled; in truth, the number of permanent converts was very small for the effort expended.

How far did religion influence the lives of women? It was said to exercise 'great influence on the Irish peasantry'. This is particularly true of women and may have deterred women from becoming involved in serious crime. The number of unmarried mothers in the country was much lower than in other countries at this time. Indeed, attitudes to sexual conduct were exceptionally strict and any manifestation of sexual interest among the young and unmarried was regarded as something to be censored and suppressed, with any lapse from virtue being severely punished. A vigilant watch was kept over the conduct of young girls. Dutton, referring to the Claddagh in 1824, stated that the residents did not want their daughters to learn English as 'they might be seduced by the soldiers'. However, not all vigilance could prevent occasional lapses: 'At wakes, not infrequently some of the young couples contrived that the place of the deceased should be supplied in a few months by a young substitute'. Married women of the county were noted for their conjugal fidelity. Women, in general, had great respect for their ministers of religion, a respect they brought with them when they emigrated. It was said of Irish Catholic emigrants in the United States in 1853, that 'they see in their priests not simple ministers of religion, but their father, their magistrate, their judge, their King, their papa, their idol'. Belief in God sustained women in their difficult lives. Religion was a very personal experience for many women, who were scrupulous about religious observance.

Some insight into the lives of the people comes from comments in parish registers, such as that of Moycullen death register. One comment there referred to the 'paucorum tantum particularium' of deaths in the parish from November 1848 to September 1849. The official number of funerals held in the church was ten between November 1848 and May 1849; however, the note proceeds: 'In hoc spatio temporis quadraginto alio, ad minimum fame pestilentia et omni genere morborum perierunt' (in this short period of time, 400 others, at least, have died of hunger, pestilence and all kinds of diseases). The tragedy continued, and entries for 1852 reveal that the Widow Cloonan died of starvation, Mary Keady of fever, while at least two people died of paralysis. The parish priest, Fr Francis Kenny, added a very interesting comment on the birth-rate in the parish: 'The births of this year exceed those of 1849 by six only. In both years they far exceeded the numbers that might be expected from the misery and physical conditions of the people. So it may be affirmed that births are not a very sure criterion of the physical comforts of the people of this country. For I have known many of these children to have been born of parents who were reduced to the last state of destitution and consequent emaciation. More generally, in the year 1849, most of them were baptised gratuitously in both years', meaning that no dues were paid for Baptisms, as the parents could not afford them.

In the immediate aftermath of the Great Famine, there seemed to be a temporary falling-off in religious practice. Wilde stated that 'The religious character of the lower Irish has received of late heavy blows, much discouragement. They are becoming irregular in many of their Church's demands on them, and they do not crowd their Churches as they used to do'. This is understandable in a people utterly drained by the calamity of the Famine. Another reason may be that the practice was no longer attended by so many of the happy customs associated with Irish religious practice earlier in the century. Sir William Wilde bemoaned their passing: 'The old forms and customs are becoming obliterated; the festivals are unobserved and the rustic festivities are neglected'. In 1849 he understood that there was 'not a candle blessed in the Chapel, nor a Brideóg seen in the Barony on Christmas Day; nor even a cock killed in every fifth house in honour of St Martin, and you'd step over the *brosnach* (firewood) of a bonfire the children lighted last St John's Eve'.

Inevitably, such changes added to the drabness of the lives of women. However, they were to take a leading part in the so-called Devotional Revolution, with extra emphasis on sodalities and confraternities from the 1850s onwards. Such devotions may have been an effort on the part of women to maintain a personal element in their devotions. Many Sacraments formerly administered in the home were now administered only in church. As far back as April 1846, for instance, one finds the following note penned in the Catholic register for the parish of Oughterard: 'From this month on, all Baptisms are to be performed in the Chapel'.

During the Famine, and in its aftermath, a wave of anti-clericalism prevailed for a time. It became fashionable in writings to attack Catholic priests. A paragraph in a New York paper read as follows:

> They (the priests) were generally accused of distributing the funds or provisions entrusted to them to those who had paid themselves best, or who, if matters should take a turn for the better, would be likely to be the most profitable sheep in their flocks.

No doubt, some instances could be found to support this statement. However, in parishes where close relationships between

[84]

priests and people had been the norm before the Famine, this relationship continued afterwards. Many women and destitute families continued to rely on the practical support of the clergy. Many emigrants sent remittances to priests to be given to their relatives. Fr Folan, a member of the Dominican community of the Claddagh, regularly did such work. For instance, one reads as follows: On 6 April 1854, Fr Folan had received £24 from former residents of the Claddagh for the purpose of assisting their relatives 'whom they left behind in absolute destitution' to emigrate to the USA: 'When the Revd Gentleman receives the cheque sent by a husband to his wife and children, he is frequently obliged to seek them out in the Poor House'. Priests resumed their efforts to provide money for the support of asylums for widows and orphans. In 1854, we read of a fund being set up for the widows and orphans of soldiers who had fought in the Crimean War, and who received no pensions. Three Dominican friars were largely instrumental in setting up this fund.

Religious acrimony continued for much of the century in the county. While evangelical efforts effected few permanent conversions, the efforts of the movement caused unfortunate long-term results. One must concur with Lecky's (1878) statement that

> Political causes, which had revived the waning antagonism between Protestants and Catholics … stimulated the spirit of proselytism and deepening religious animosities and added greatly to the social and political divisions of the nation.

There was no noticeable difference in attitude to women in the practices of the Roman Catholic, Church of Ireland and other Protestant denominations. In all of them, women played a subservient role in organisations run along patriarchal lines.

EDUCATION

Education in nineteenth-century Ireland must be viewed against a very troubled political and social background. In the early part of the century, there was a bewildering array of schools funded in various ways, in the absence of a centralised education system, but large areas of many counties, including Galway, had no schools at all; many people, received no formal education.

Although the Act of Union (1800) was followed by a growing state interest in providing mass popular education, the poor received little education in either town or country prior to 1831 despite attempts made by organisations and individuals to set up schools, funded in different ways. Several parish schools were supported by Roman Catholic parishioners; a large number were supported by Protestant education societies, sometimes called bible societies, such as the London Hibernian Society; a smaller number were supported by landlords, such as Miss Netterfield at Clonkeen in the barony of Tiaquin. Several girls were taught in the Female Free School in Tuam, supported by the proceeds of charity balls. Some schools filled particular social needs; thus, before the Famine, Miss Jean Trench of Woodlawn ran a private school, which equipped girls for British colonial life.

While Parliament had granted aid to the Kildare Place Society from 1811 onwards to provide opportunities for education for members of the lower classes, it was not until 1831, that Stanley, the Chief Secretary, set about establishing a national system of primary education, a move which was to have far-reaching effects on the lives of young girls and women in the country. Clergymen, including some Presbyterians and a few influential Roman Catholic clergymen, objected to the new system for several reasons, mainly pertaining to questions of control of schools and possible proselytism. Concessions granted initially to Presbyterians 'gradually led to a system which was *de facto*, denominational'. Some Catholic bishops also opposed the scheme. Poor Catholic clergymen, however, willingly accepted government grants to found schools, many in new 'chapel villages'. Many villages were founded, under the patronage of substantial farmers and merchants after the granting of Catholic Emancipation (1829). Many Catholic priests became patrons of national schools, applying for schools and becoming their managers; they frequently placed existing schools under the National Board; among them were two charity schools in Galway, one run by the Presentation Sisters. By there were 115 national schools in the county. This was a major improvement, as areas such as Ardrahan, Kiltartan, Clonfert, Ballymacward and the town of Ballinasloe had no national schools in 1835; side-by-side with the national schools, private schools, even hedge-schools, were still being founded in that year, for example in Kilcolgan. However, as the national schools became more widespread, primary education became standardised with many private schools either closing or being amalgamated with primary schools. A common curriculum came to be followed and so began the era of universal literacy in the country.

The main thrust in education was centred on primary education. The Kildare Commission (1854) examined the possibility of establishing a public system of intermediate education on the existing endowments of endowed schools. Because existing funds were insufficient for such a system, they recommended a national system under local management. This was but one of many attempts to set up a system of intermediate education, which did not really get under way until the Intermediate Education Act (1878), the terms of which initially applied to boys only. However, even before Catholic Emancipation (1829), some Sisters provided intermediate education for girls although progress was very slow. In 1871, in Galway City, for instance, there were five all-male superior schools, one mixed male and female school, and no all-girls superior school. (A superior school taught one or more foreign languages.) A mere 50 girls as against 372 boys, received secondary education in the town in that year. Of the 50 girls, 22 were in private Catholic schools. No Protestant or Episcopalian girl attended the superior schools of the town; however, many girls from well-to-do families were either taught at home by governesses or attended schools overseas. Some elements of secondary education were sometimes provided within the national school system. Ironically, the system displaced teachers who operated private pay schools, where both elementary and secondary education were provided. Later, the Powis Commission did not favour the extension of the primary school course to intermediate subjects. Despite some well-meaning efforts, few girls received secondary education until the beginning of the twentieth century.

Workhouse schools are of great interest because of the huge numbers of children in them. At the end of 1850, there were 119,628 children under 15 in workhouses; in April 1851, there were still 106,000, 40% of whom were orphaned or deserted and almost 50% were illegitimate children accompanied by their mothers. The education afforded to these children was coloured by the nineteenth century attitude to the education of the poor, which deemed that their education should fit them for useful manual work as labourers or domestic servants. In 1831, the Commissioners of National Education offered assistance to the Boards of Guardians. They proposed to teach children of different creeds together and show that the system had adapted itself to Irish conditions; in theory, workhouse schools would be subject to the Board's inspection and religious proselytism forbidden. The Commissioners ordered that a schoolmaster and mistress were to be appointed to the workhouse of the most populous Unions. In other Unions, children attended national schools at first. By 1842, many Unions operated schools in association with the Commissioners and within four years, workhouse schools numbered 99. The workhouse school in Clifden was attended by 60 boys and 240 girls (all inmates) all neatly dressed and carefully disciplined and taught. However, most Boards of Guardians were unwilling to allow workhouse children attend national schools, to be taught by teachers who were not under the authority of the Guardians or central authority. In practice, the Commissioners had little input in workhouse school management as the Guardians both selected teachers and fixed their salaries, which varied considerably from Union to Union.

Educational standards in many schools were deplorable. Regulations for workhouse schools specified that children should receive three hours instruction daily (six hours were specified for ordinary national schools). The curriculum comprised of reading, writing, arithmetic and religious knowledge and occupational instruction 'to fit the children for service'. The children were disadvantaged by overcrowded classes. All tuition was through English and no Irish-speaking teachers were appointed. Reputable teachers would not work in such schools: 'such work was repugnant to the common feelings of man', as teachers were frequently compelled to work as ward-attendants and storekeepers as well as teach and their work was of low status.

Vocational training was the only item stressed by many Guardians, who felt that the industrial training of girls in the workhouses was comparatively an easy task, 'as the domestic and economic duties of the house itself functioned as a means of employing them in almost all occupations which will hereafter fall to their lot in private life'. The Revd S.G. Osborne, in his *Gleanings in the West of Ireland* (1850), explained the practical difficulties of providing industrial training, with particular reference to Tuam Workhouse: 'There is not room to afford the space for any real amount of industrial occupation: there is only one-tenth of the staff required to secure it'. At times, a philanthropist, such as Golding Bird in Galway, helped to secure industrial employment for workhouse children, especially girls. Conditions varied greatly from one workhouse to another. In 1848, conditions in the Galway Girls school were excellent; which was unusual. Despite the help available from the Commissioners, many schools were neglected and without books; among them was the Female School of Loughrea Workhouse in 1848, where no kind of industrial instruction was given. Greater efforts were made at times to run the boys' schools efficiently, while neglecting the girls. In Clifden, the girls' school had been converted to a washroom, while the boys' was well conducted. Much depended on school staff. In June 1848, it was reported that 'in Loughrea, conditions previously notorious had improved under the care of an efficient and useful schoolmistress, making bonnets for the inmates'.

Because of the numbers of girls in workhouses and the demand for servants in the colonies, the Commissioners regarded organised emigration as an acceptable answer to the problem of large numbers of girls and young women in workhouses. On 22 October 1849, the Poor Law Guardians addressed a circular to each Board of Guardians, calling attention to regulations previously issued with special reference to girls and to the importance of maintaining a regular system of instruction and employment of the girls in household and domestic work, as far as practicable in such establishments. The following year, teachers were reminded of the necessity of giving instruction 'as shall fit the inmates for service and train them to habits of usefulness, industry and virtue'. Matrons and Masters were also reminded of their duties, with particular reference to the industrial training of girls. The Commissioners stated that girls desirous of emigrating

> should be selected according to their conduct and suitable-ness as emigrants and the progress they had made in those industrial acquirements which are likely to enable them to earn their own livelihood in the countries to which they may be sent.

Some critics, including Osborne, castigated the workhouse regime. He spoke of between 700 and 800 'Workhouse mermaids vegetating in idleness' in Galway Auxiliary Workhouse, whose lives did not fit them for emigration: 'A female colonist should be brought up hardily in habits of industry, adept in that kind of mixed labour (which would fit them) for out-of-door service, marriage or life in the bush'. Not everybody agreed with him. At this time, there was a demand for female servants, especially in Canada. A report from Canada stated that the young females sent out by the unions of Galway and Clifden were remarkable for their clean healthy condition, the habits of discipline acquired in the unions being of great service'.

How many young people emigrated from workhouses?

*Return of Emigrants sent out or assisted to emigrate by Boards of Guardians
in Ireland, in pursuance of the provisions of the Irish Poor Relief Act*

Years ended 1st March	No. of Unions	Numbers sent, being Fifteen years of age, and upwards		Childen under fifteen years of age	Total
		Males	Females		
1850	18	201	400	270	871
1851	52	360	844	517	1,721
1852	79	790	2,644	952	4,386
1853	93	492	2,218	1,115	3,825
1854	90	403	1,202	996	2,601
1855	103	159	2,847	788	3,794
1856	86	64	363	403	830
1857	81	76	363	363	802
1858	84	58	469	302	829
1859	66	37	270	180	487
1860	68	45	178	141	364
1861	70	44	178	125	347
1862	38	12	72	38	122
1863	64	41	317	139	497

Up to 1855 it was the disaster of 1845–9 which was working itself out in emigration. There was a sudden collapse in numbers after 1855, which saw a general fall both in the numbers in workhouses and the numbers emigrating from them, although the numbers of girls outnumbered the boys sent overseas up to 1872. The Poor Law Commissioners regarded the scheme of sending young boys and girls from the workhouses to overseas colonies as a success as it had relieved the public at home from a serious financial burden, while simultaneously benefitting the colonies and enabling the emigrants to follow a useful, respectable career.

Workhouse schools were usually segregated. Galway City had one all-male and one all-female workhouse school. In 1871, there were 46 boys and 25 girls in these schools, all Roman Catholics, between the ages of seven and 16. In that year, no provision was made for secondary education of any type in these schools.

The Kildare Place Society began formal teacher training in Ireland in 1814 for males, (1824 for females), and trained 2,500 teachers between 1814 and 1831. On the successful completion of the training programme of 7–8 weeks, three categories of certificate were granted, 'competent', 'fully competent', and 'having had an opportunity of becoming acquainted with the system'. Trainee teachers were aged between 16 and 50. A training college for male national teachers was opened in Marlborough Street, Dublin, in 1838 and one for women in 1842. These were known as Normal Establishments. Model schools were also set up, where candidate teachers were trained by laymen, without supervision by the church authorities. The curriculum in girls' model schools was centred on the domestic sphere with needle-work as a core subject. Needlework was upgraded in 1846 to include domestic economy, simple cookery, laundry and household management. The training course lasted for six months. After 1849, these colleges received many high-achieving pupils from the model schools. Some trainee teachers were former monitor pupils selected by inspectors in the ordinary national schools.

The monitor system is of great interest. Monitors were 'pupils who for some period each day helped with the teaching'. A junior monitor, aged 11, was appointed for three years. At the end of that period, if considered satisfactory, he/she could become a senior monitor and serve for a further period of four years. At the end of 1851, there were eight paid male and four female monitors in each district. On reaching 18, a monitor might apply for an appointment as a pupil teacher in a district model school for a period or two years. The monitor training scheme was further extended in 1863. In a few very large, highly-efficient schools, such as the Mercy Primary School in Gort, the Commissioners appoint-ed young persons of great merit to act as First-Class Monitors on a new higher salary scale. In Gort, in 1864, 11 female monitor pupils were being instructed by one of the six teaching Sisters. This development gave a certain limited recognition to some large convent schools as training schools, of the same status as the district model schools. Such training led in time to the feminisation of the teaching profession in Ireland at primary school level, as they trained far more lady teachers than the colleges run by the Commissioners of National Education. A special class of teacher, 15 male and 15 female remained in the National Teacher Training Colleges for five years and were selected from the best students who had passed through the ordinary training course. This special class received extra daily instruction from the professors and undertook practice teaching in the model schools.

The Powis Commission (1870), however, disapproved of the model schools as teacher training centres, as they were schools of intermediate instruction for the middle and professional classes and not schools for the poor. The Catholic bishops sought to establish Catholic training colleges as did other religious denominations. Both denominational and interdenominational training colleges had been founded in England in 1840. Finally, Catholic training colleges were opened in Dublin in the 1880s.

The need for teacher training was great. Even national schools employed some untrained teachers. Several schools were closed at times, because of the scarcity of trained teachers, particularly in the early years of the national system. In time, the Board exerted pressure on teachers to obtain teaching qualifications within a specified period. In July 1855 in Boula National School, Miss E. Clarke, had been employed as a teacher for seven years. The manager wished to retain her services, contrary to the Commissioners' order of dismissal, dated 18 July 1855, which the Commissioners refused to rescind, as 'she has been above seven years in the Board's service without obtaining classification, a fact in itself sufficient to prove her utter incompetence'. On obtaining classification, one still had to take examinations to retain one's status. Failure to pass these might constitute grounds for dismissal. Miss Honoria Lyons, who taught at Kilcooley Female National School, Roll No. 6561 was dismissed for insufficient answering in the general examinations in Ballinasloe in 1857. She may have been a poor examination candidate but a capable, practical teacher as her applications for employment were supported by both the school manager and the local schools inspector. Previously, on 8 September 1854, a teacher had been dismissed from her post in this school because she was 'unfit to conduct a school of this description'. It was stated that there would be no objection made to her appointment as a 'teacher of a national school of an inferior class'. The manager of this school was unable to employ a competent successor for some time. The problem of untrained teachers was an ongoing one and in 1874 about one-third of the country's teachers were still without formal teacher training. The problem continued into the twentieth century and was resolved only with much difficulty.

The vexed question of curriculum exercised the minds of educationalists in Ireland. The *Galway Patriot* of 13 September for instance referred to 'Hedge Teachers with their 3Rs in their windows reading, wrighting and arithmetic', adding that a penny a week would be charged for 'them as learns Grammar'. Most schools taught basic reading, writing and arithmetic. In schools, where arithmetic or mathematics were not taught, teachers were predominantly women and they could be found both in rural and urban districts. In 1835, for example, the Loughrea Boarding and Day Female School taught English, French, drawing and needle-work. Sunday schools, as at Aughrim, taught spelling, reading and religious instruction.

Great emphasis was placed on vocational training for both boys and girls. In the Presentation Convent Schools in Galway, renowned for training girls in making lace and shawls, three hours daily were devoted to reading, writing and arithmetic and the remaining three hours were devoted to lace-making. Industrial Schools under the control of the Board of Education were required to spend only two hours daily on literary work and four hours on industrial training. In the Girls Industrial School in Clifden, where the girls were taught useful household arts (washing, making and mending), those who showed a special aptitude were trained for work as shop assistants. In national schools, the Board encouraged the teaching of agriculture and gardening to boys and girls; it was their stated intention to produce an 'intelligent class of farm labourers and servants'. The Board also allowed for subjects, for which there was a particular local demand, such as navigation in Claddagh, and stressed the teaching of needlework, which met with the parents' approval: 'the practical knowledge of needlework ... very useful to females generally and particularly so to the humbler classes, whether applied to domestic purposes, or as a mode of remunerative employment'. The Commissioners reported, however, in 1898, that despite their best efforts, domestic economy was confined mainly to convent national schools and to practising schools of the training college for females. As a reaction to this report, they ordered that a minimum of one hour daily should be devoted to needlework from 1890 onwards. All was not seriousness, however; dancing was popular and parents were willing to pay so that their children would be properly taught. Mrs Blake, in her *Letters from the Irish Highlands* (1825), disapproved of the poor spending hard-earned tenpennies on dancing masters.

An examination of the Regulations and Curriculum of the Dominican Convent Superior School (A Superior school taught at least one foreign language) in Taylor's Hill, Galway reveal both its ethos and curriculum. The Regulations stated:

> Each young lady to approach the Sacrament of Penance once a month.
>
> Out of school no pupil is to associate with a companion unless she have the sanction of her parents and the religious.
>
> Each child to be provided with work materials, books, according to the list; and no one is to lend or borrow from another.
>
> Silence to be observed during school hours.
>
> Shoes to be changed before entering the school room and each pupil to be particular in making her salutation. (Polite greetings were the order of the day)
>
> The lessons marked to be well studied at home and music pupils to practise one hour daily.

In 1858, the curriculum was set out as follows:

DAILY DUTIES:	Religious Instruction, English Reading, Parsing, Dictation, Needlework, Tables

ALTERNATE DUTIES:

Monday, Wednesday, Friday:	Grammar, Arithmetic, History, Chronology, French Conversation
Tuesday, Thursday, Saturday:	Sacred History, Geography, Spelling, Mythology, French Dictation

Monday	English Letter
Tuesday	Object Lesson
Wednesday	Natural History
Thursday	Astronomy
Friday	–
Saturday	Long Religious Instruction

This plan had to be modified, as the pupils were 'too backward for such a course'. Such a wide-ranging curriculum was rare. There was an on-going debate about which subjects should be taught to girls, and there was much sex-stereotyping in the curriculum. The Master of Galway Workhouses, however, recommended sewing, washing and spinning for girls to make them good servants and enable them to earn their living respectably; he felt that these subjects were more useful to girls than Geography. He argued that boys needed such subjects (perhaps to enable them to obtain one of the wider range of jobs available to at least some boys), but girls should be trained as good housewives. Not all Guardians agreed with this widely-held opinion. Mark Lynch, the High Sheriff, stressed the importance for girls of a good general education, to enable them to obtain positions as governesses. In the *Galway Advertiser* in 1847 a young lady seeking a post as governess stated: 'She will be competent in English and French education, music, writing, history, geography, etc., also plain and fancy needlework'.

There was a 'hidden curriculum' in operation with reference to girls' subjects. Girls were expected to study a limited range of subjects to accomplishment level only, with the sole exception of household management, where 'formal training in the household chores would make women content as housewives by teaching them the challenges in traditional responsibilities'. Ambition was frowned on: 'knowledge was to teach her (a girl) to know her place and her functions: to make her content with the one and willing to fulfil the other'.

Religious instruction caused much controversy. The religious acrimony, which poisoned so many aspects of Irish life, also permeated its classrooms. Society in Ireland was organised on narrrow denominational lines, with each denomination distrustful of the other; few people saw the desirability of mixed schooling. Boys and girls were usually segregated in religious instruction classes. In practice, a great variety in the pattern of religious instruction prevailed, even in hedgeschools. Some gave no religious instruction whatever, as at Clontuskert; others, which had both Protestant and Catholic children, taught separate Catechisms. The Church of Ireland and Dissenters provided religious instruction in Sunday Schools, which had 160 schools in Connacht in 1841, employing 686 teachers. Women played an active part in this work, including Mrs Mary Browne 'foundress' of St Nicholas Sunday School in Galway City, whose achievements are honoured by a plaque in St Nicholas Collegiate Church. The national school system, for its part, aimed to keep religious and secular instruction separate:

> No child shall be required to be present at any religious instruction of which his parents or guardians may disapprove and opportunities shall be afforded to all children to receive separately, at particular periods, such religious instruction as their parents or guardians may provide for them. One day, at least, in each week (independently of Sunday) is to be set apart for the religious instruction of the children.

Despite their best efforts, the Commissioners failed to keep religious and secular instruction apart. They were themselves partly to blame: their textbooks for combined instruction were full of material that, although technically neutral as between denominations, was bound to raise religious instructions.

Protestant educators were dissatisfied with the Board's provisions for religious instruction. The Irish Church Education Society, founded in 1838, insisted that all children in their schools must read the Bible. The Society made substantial progress in the archdiocese of Tuam, as parents reacted to a row, caused by religious bigotry, between Archbishop John MacHale and the Commissioners. The archbishop disapproved of both mixed education and the national system, which he described in 1838 as narrow, bigoted and insulting and he asserted that he would not allow schools in his diocese to be bound by some of its rules. Thus began a long controversy. In 1839, all schools under Catholic management in the archdiocese severed connections with the National Board (on the orders of the archbishop) with dire results for primary education in many parts of the archdiocese. By late 1840, there were only 12 Catholic schools open there; these were ones which had Protestant managers or patrons who did not feel bound by the archbishop's commands. As a result of the archbishop's actions, more proselytising agencies established themselves in the archdiocese than in most areas in Ireland. They set up schools, generally in areas where there were no national schools. Many Catholics deplored MacHale's attitude; for them, the national school system gave them freedom of choice and lessened the appeal of the free education provided by the Bible schools. Their attitude was essentially pragmatic. Some continued to send children to school; others felt bound by the strictures of the archbishop. The net result was that very many children in the diocese were educationally deprived.

Ironically, despite the acrimony which religious instruction caused, little or no religious instruction was given in many schools, including national schools in both rural and urban areas. In 1835, in Ballinakill, only one of its schools provided religious instruction. In nearby Ballinasloe, of six schools, one gave no religious instruction, two used both Roman Catholic and Protestant catechisms and the other three used Roman Catholic catechisms. It is evident that a wide variety of instructional practice prevailed. Sadly, the school situation both reflected and reinforced the widespread religious hostility in society.

Of interest is the role played by the primary school system in the decline of the Irish language and the spread of English. Frequently, primary schools have often been condemned for the destruction of the Irish language, but, in fact, English was the medium of instruction in most schools, long before the national schools, which served as a mechanism for furthering a pre-existing trend, not as a primary cause of the trend. Most Irish people wanted their children to speak and read English, particularly as Irish had become associated with poverty long before the Famine. Many parents were anxious that their children learn English, whether to assist them as emigrants, or as a means of obtaining employment, such as the Civil Service, the Royal Irish Constabulary or, in the case of girls, teaching and the post office. In areas, where the teaching of English met with opposition, other factors operated, such as the fear that it might lead to the break-up of closely-knit communities, such as the Claddagh, who 'held little or no intercourse with others, marrying only amongst themselves'. Knowledge of English frequently conferred status on speakers; in the West of Ireland, such girls and women wore ribbons in their caps as a badge of status.

Unfortunately, Irish was not used as a medium of instruction for many years and few Irish-speaking teachers were appointed to the schools until the late nineteenth century. Census figures recorded that in 1851, 23.3% of the population of Ireland was unable to speak English, 19.1% in 1861 and 15.1% in 1871. In 1851, there was a majority of those who spoke Irish only in three of the eighteen baronies of the county – Clare, Moycullen and Ross. There was no clear over-all picture of the bilingual speakers. In the county as a whole, almost 25% spoke Irish only; in Galway city, 14.75% of the population. In most baronies, there were more bilingual men than women. Such a widespread knowledge of English cannot be ascribed solely to the national schools; it reflects the desire of parents and society that young people should know English. Sadly, the concept of promoting both languages was not considered, thus depriving many young people of the rich heritage of their ancestral language.

The development of segregated schooling in the 1830s is of interest. Hedgeschools traditionally were non-segregated and in rural areas several primary schools began as mixed schools. When pupil numbers increased, it was customary, however, to found separate girls' schools. This trend also applied in Technical Schools run by religious, near the end of the century, as at Portumna and in Teacher Training Colleges. Class segregation also operated in schools; frequently, a two-tiered system operated, where fees paid by pupils in pay schools subsidised schools for the poor. In Clifden, for example, the Sisters of Mercy, opened both a pay school and a poor school in 1863. Many poor schools were, in fact, modelled on tne French *ouvroirs* of the seventeenth and eighteenth centuries, where poor female children learned to work, read and write and were given a grounding in Catholic doctrine. Arguments about relevance, based on Utilitarian philosophy, were on-going. Thus, the Select Committee of 1838 called for a comprehensive primary school curriculum, more utilitarian and practical, relating to the economic needs of the community. Later, a Royal Commission (1855) called for curriculum expansion and reform. It found

> a need for intermediate education, not only in the Classics and mathematics, English language and literature, foreign languages and experimental and natural sciences, book-keeping, drawing and singing.

Many convents founded training departments aided by the Science and Art Department of South Kensington, London. Private school teachers followed the curriculum of their alma mater; one such was Miss Maxey, who founded a young ladies' school in Galway in 1831; her system of tuition being based on that of

Winchester Convent, where she had been educated. As the century progressed, both school curricula and examination systems were regularised.

The benefits of an improved school system were frequently negated by poor school attendance, often caused by distance from school, poor clothing and poverty. The cost of tuition was about a penny a week in most pay schools. A labourer's daily wage ranged between six and ten pence and thus schools fees represented a huge financial sacrifice for many parents. Pre-Famine school enrolments may be gleaned from various sources:

Year	Numbers enrolled at school	Population in millions
1821	394,813	6.8
1834	633,946	7.9
1841	502,950	8.2

Sources: 1821 Census (P.P. 1824 xxii) p. 817; Second Report of the Commissioners of Public Instruction (Ireland), P.P. 1835 xxxiv p. 13; 1841 Census pp 438–9

Some of these figures are a rough estimate as few schools kept accurate Registers before 1831. To complicate matters, pre–1841 data includes a small, unspecified number of pupils in Industrial Schools.

Mixed schools had a larger male than female enrolment, whether in towns, such as Loughrea or rural areas, such as Kilkerrin. Enrolment increased by 10% in Galway between 1841 and 1851 but dropped by 16% in Galway city in the same period. The drop in enrolments was noted in other large centres of population at this time, such as Cork and may be ascribed to poverty and the ravages of the Famine. The increase in the county may perhaps be attributed to the increased number of national schools.

Poor school attendance was particularly noticeable, especially in winter, when as many as half of those enrolled stayed at home. The Powis Commission (1870) calculated that for Ireland as a whole, 33.5% of pupils had an annual attendance of 100 days or less. The Commission recommended a system of payments by results and expressed its dissatisfaction with school attendance and children's proficiency. It was not until 1883 that the principle of compulsory education was accepted. School attendance was finally made compulsory in Ireland in 1892 with the passing of the Irish Education Act, which also specified acceptable excuses for non-attendance, such as sickness or harvesting operations. School attendance was greatly affected in rural areas by farm work in spring and autumn. It was less affected by migration as many migrants would normally have left school; for example, in summer 1841, 57,000 harvest migrants left Irish ports for main-land Britain, 87% of whom were males aged 16–35. There was no capitation system of grants payable to schools and conse-quently no inducement to enforce school attendance. Societal attitudes to girls also affected attendance patterns: Dutton, in the 1820s, spoke of girls being removed from school 'as soon as they were able to soften the labours of their mothers'. However, the pattern of attendance and attainment for girls changed over time particularly after the Famine. David Fitzpatrick (1986) has argued that the superior performance of girls reflected not only their possibly stronger desire to better themselves, but their declining importance in the labour market, particularly in rural areas, where the female contribution to farm work diminished during the century. Some parents may have been more than willing to educate girls to make them employable. One cannot but concur with the statement that 'even in Ireland, utility sometimes outweighed prejudice'. During the Famine, school attendance in some areas was linked to relief provision, in the form of food. The British Relief Association required children to attend school in order to obtain relief. They unwittingly damaged the cause of education, as several children attended school under the pretext of education. They regarded education as bribery and promptly left school, when charity came to an end.

School appointments were linked to school attendance even before schooling became compulsory. An application from Castle

Hacket (No. 4216) on 18 April 1850 for a Workmistress was rejected, as the average female attendance for the six months previous to the Inspector's visit was insufficient.

What educational standards were attained? In 1841, only 28% of Ireland's population, 5 years and upwards could read and write, in 1871, it was 49% and in 1881, 59%. Connacht was the slowest to make progress and in 1841, only 16% of the population could read and write. The following figures for Galway county and city reveal comparative figures for 1841 and 1851. Figures for Galway City reveal a decline in the figures for both men and women who could read and write in the decade. The spread of literacy could not be wholly ascribed to the spread of the national schools; there was a gradual improvement between the 1780s and 1830s, although the main spread came with the spread of the national schools.

Many children attended school until they mastered the Second Book, one of a series of recommended books which

Persons five years old and upwards who could read and write				
	Male	Male	Female	Female
	1841	1851	1841	1851
Galway County	20%	25%	8%	13%
Galway City	43%	39%	25%	22%
Percentage of persons five years old and upwards who could read and write				
	1841	1851	1841	1851
Galway County	9%	10%	8%	10%
Galway City	10%	13%	15%	15%
Percentage of persons five years and upwards who could neither read nor write				
	1841	1851	1841	1851
Galway County	71%	65%	84%	77%
Galway City	47%	48%	60%	63%

Source: 1851 Census Table xxvi

formed a logical, integrated sequence of instruction, taking the child from elementary literacy to fairly sophisticated lessons in geography, science and literature'. The fourth and fifth books contained material of secondary-school level; thus, a pupil could receive the basis of a secondary education in the local national school, given the good fortune of a competent teacher and of parents who allowed him/her to remain in school. Some incentives operated to retain pupils in school. Brighter pupils aimed to become first monitors and then teachers. Girls sought posts as shop assistants or in the Post Office. In the schools for the poor, many children received both food and clothing. Schools with Industrial Training Departments were popular, as they taught survival skills and pupils were allowed to retain the proceeds of the sale of some of the school's manufactured work. Others sought a basic standard of literacy before emigrating. Some girls were apprenticed to trades. For boys, there was possible admission to the University Colleges, such as Trinity College, Dublin or one of the new Queen's Colleges in Dublin, Belfast, Cork or Galway, the police or the Civil Service. After the Great Famine, parents were particularly anxious that, where possible, their sons would obtain permanent, pensionable positions. There were fewer posts of this type for girls.

What of the teachers themselves? What were their lives like? Teachers both in private and public schools were inadequately paid. In 1847, the Commissioners of National Education admitted that teachers' salaries were inadequate to secure the permanent services of good teachers. In 1848, the salary of a national school teacher was 'utterly inadequate to his social position and requirements and calculated to restrict the influence of his teaching and example by degrading him as a citisen and member of the community'. This was even more pertinent in the case of women teachers, who received less than their male counterparts at all points of the scale. In 1851, primary school teachers' salaries were as follows:

First class	Males	Females
	£ per annum	£ per annum
1st Division	35	24
2nd Division	28	20
3rd Division	24	18
Second Class	Males	Females
1 st Division	21	16
2nd Division	19	15
Third Class	Males	Females
First Division	17	14
Second Division	15	13

In 1857, increases were granted as follows:

	Old Scale		New Scale	
First Class	Male	Female	Male	Female
	£ per annum	£ per annum	£ per annum	£ per annum
1st Division	36	25	46	36
2nd Division	30	22	38	30
3rd Division	25	19	32	24
Second Class	Male	Female	Male	Female
1st Division	22	17	26	22
2nd Division	20	16	24	10
Third Class	Male	Female	Male	Female
1st Division	18	15	20	17
2nd Division	15	13	17	15

Teachers of needlework who worked part-time were paid £6 per annum. Some increases were granted over the years. In 1857, all ranks with the exception of teachers of needlework received increased payments. These increases ranged from 13% to 30%. However, even in 1868, the average pay of the national school teacher was about one-third that of teachers in England. Many teachers were so poor that they were compelled to accept relief during the Great Famine; others died of fever caught in their schools; some who could afford the fare emigrated to the USA. Public opinion did not support increases in teachers' salaries. In public disquiet about proposed salary increases was voiced:

> Teachers should remain prizes for the poor, not for the rich. Teachers should not be made into fine gentlemen (or ladies, presumably) or raised to an eminence so high as to dissipate all affinity between them and the parents of their pupils.

Despite poor pay and conditions, teaching posts were eagerly sought after, particularly those in model schools. The school mistress in Galway Model School was paid a salary of £55 per annum in 1851 and also received half of the school fees. Teachers in workhouse schools were not so fortunate. In 1847, in recognition of the poor salaries paid to them, a scheme to award annual gratuities to the most deserving was inaugurated. In 1850, Margaret Moriarty of Clifden Workhouse received a gratuity of £1.10s. for 'attention to her duties, and the highly satisfactory manner in which her school was conducted'. Working conditions were generally deplorable. Teachers could be dismissed very readily and salaries withheld on the whim of a manager. Teachers' residences were provided from 1872 in some areas; a Teachers Pension Scheme was founded in 1879.

Obtaining an appointment as a teacher could be quite difficult. For example, to get sanction for a needlework teacher, the school manager had to apply on a special form, which gave the name and age of the teacher and supplied answers to the following queries:

1 What testimonials can she produce of fitness for her office as work mistress?

2 Is she to be employed exclusively in teaching needlework?

3 Specify the different kinds of needlework which it is proposed she will teach.

4 Is instruction in needlework to be given in the ordinary classroom or in a separate apartment?

5 If in the classroom, what are the dimensions of it in the clear?

6 Has a convenient work table been provided?

7 Has a press for holding work also been provided? (20th Report 1846)

Many schools failed to meet this criteria and appointments were not made despite the popularity of needlework as a subject.

The education system set up in the nineteenth century served the country well; among some of the most far-reaching changes in Irish education, which had been accomplished by the end of the century, was the increased school enrolment and attendance of girls, and the foundation of congregations of teaching sisters. They, and members of other religious groups, saw the training of young girls as of paramount importance, particularly those who were poor. They aimed at 'permanent relief' (paid employment), as they were aware of the unemployment and underemployment which afflicted them. They thus continued the links between schools and industrial training and job creation, availing of the provisions of the Technical Instruction Act to obtain extra resources.

In ordinary life, literacy greatly influenced women's lives. Emigrants' letters revealed a new world with employment prospects overseas. At home literacy affected consumption patterns. The later nineteenth century saw the widespread popularity of mail-order catalogues and the purchase of articles of clothing from England, facilitated by the spread of post office services, especially the introduction of a parcel service. Literacy gave people access to a world of literature previously unknown.

The largest change in Irish education, particularly for women, was that very many people now had access to education. At the beginning of the century it could be stated that 'most Irish women experienced neither education nor emigration'. The end of the century was conspicuous by their experience of both.

3

Distress

Provisions for the relief of distress were of great importance because of the endemic poverty and the number of famines throughout the century. Throughout the period, many of the poor were dependent on charity administered by the churches and voluntary subscriptions. In fact, Church of Ireland parishes had played an active part in poor relief, giving alms to the chronically poor and organising local relief committees in bad years, over a 200-year period; Catholic priests took up special collections and donated the proceeds of charity sermons to support long-term projects and provide emergency relief. Usually, Protestant and Catholic clergy worked together in times of crisis to provide relief.

The problem of poverty exercised many minds in the first half of the century; in 1831, Chief Secretary Stanley set up Boards of Education and Public Works to alleviate poverty. Later, in 1838, the Poor Law was extended to Ireland in an effort to provide permanent official relief. This law, as applied to Ireland, differed from that in England in significant ways, which were to have important long-term effects on the working of the Poor Law in Ireland, particularly during the Great Famine. These differences may be summarised as follows:

1   Outdoor relief was absolutely forbidden; all relief was to be channelled through the workhouse, as the government wished to keep permanent relief confined to the work-

houses. Thus, despite the Act of Union in 1800, the provisions of the 1842 Outdoor Relief Act were not extended to Ireland.

2 No right to relief existed; if a workhouse was full, the Guardians were not obliged to provide any other form of relief for the destitute.

3 Paupers did not have to have lived in a particular area in order to obtain relief. (Kinealy, 1997)

The Poor Law, as applied to Ireland, helped to break up the fabric of rural society as 'most of the Irish who threw up their land to enter the workhouses, threw up all hope of re-entering their own economy; if they clung to it, the problem would remain untouched for a time, until masses of them broke under some sudden strain and overwhelmed the meagre workhouse system', originally designed to hold 80,000–100,000 people.

The 'sudden strain' was the Great Famine, the greatest of many nineteenth-century famines. This famine, sometimes called the Great Hunger, struck suddenly, ironically in a year when the crop ('the poor man's property') was never so large or abundant. At first, people did not panic, hoping that the blight which spread unevenly over the country like a scourge of locusts in 1845 would not recur. People were accustomed to lean years, death and fever when the potato crop failed; in fact, over half the potato crops between 1816 and 1842 had been complete and partial failures, caused by diseases (such as curl), and bad weather. Their hopes were dashed, however, as the blight struck Ireland for seven consecutive years, although its incidence was localised in some years. Hardship was also aggravated by unusually severe weather and fuel shortages during the same period. In 1845, attempts were made to provide relief when the extent of the blight became known. A few landlords reduced rents on conacre quite considerably; the *Galway Vindicator* of 2 December 1845 stated that Oliver Jackson in Tuam reduced the rent of a conacre field near the town from £4 10s. to £2 and Mr Connor Kelly of Coalpark also granted a similar reduction. The Mansion House Committee, which was to provide sterling service in relief operations for the rest of the century, was founded in Dublin in late 1845. Peel's government reacted quickly; his efforts were delayed by the inaction of officials in Dublin Castle, who expected that 1846 would produce a good crop of potatoes. Peel introduced a package of relief measures; he aimed to provide short-term relief and repeal the corn laws as a long-term aim. Loans were given to set up public works; the population of Cashla, Lettermore and Garumna Island were completely dependent on them for relief. The public works were to be paid for by Grand Jury cess, a tax levied on occupiers of land. People looked forward to getting on the public works, although they recognised that abuses attached to them. Public works had, in fact, been used to provide relief in earlier famines, such as that of 1831. Peel, unofficially, imported corn into the country in an attempt to keep down food prices. While maize or Indian meal had been imported into Ireland since the earlier part of the century, that imported by Peel came to be known as 'Peel's brimstone', despised at first by those who had no experience of it. Many women did not know how to cook maize, others had no proper utensils to do so. During the bitter winter of 1845 people looked forward to a good potato crop in 1846 and the possibility of obtaining outdoor relief, particularly when rumours spread that food depots were to be opened in 1846, including one in Galway.

In June 1846, Peel resigned and was succeeded by Russell. Like Peel, Russell did not close the ports, which had been done in times of crisis even in the eighteenth century; neither did his government import food to keep down the food prices in the market. Russell's government relied on a system of public works, which were designed to transfer responsibility for all relief to the Poor Law. While women looked forward to obtaining assistance through employment on the public works, most of them were to be sadly disappointed. Few of them obtained employment on public works, which generally consisted of building roads, such as Grattan Road in Galway. In October 1846, there were 625 men on the public works in Galway, and a mere 11 women. In November

21: Garumna Island: dinner on Indian meal supplied
by a relief committee

1847, the number of women had increased to 69 in Galway. Of
interest is the fact that almost seven times as many were employed
in nearby County Mayo during the same period. The rate of
daily wages on public works was pitched at less than the average
local wage, in an attempt to discourage prospective applicants for
relief. At the same time, no effort was made to control prices.
Thus, retail corn prices rose from £11 to £17–£18 per ton
between the beginning and end of September 1846. In the same
month, the Board of Works attempted to substitute a system of
task labour to eliminate the 'general indolence involved in daily
wage rates' (some Board of Works supervisors felt that workers
did minimum work for daily wage rates and they felt that
productivity could be measured and improved by setting task
work); this new system operated to the general detriment of the

sick, the infirm, the aged poor, women and adolescents. One is not therefore surprised to find that along the Western seaboard, malnourished people melted away like snow in the sun and the living were marked by fatalism and passivity during the grim winter of 1846–7, when the blizzards, which so cruelly affected Northern Europe, caused great hardship in Ireland. The provision of public works depended to a great extent on local property owners being in a position to provide collateral security for the money advanced for such schemes. The people of Spiddal were barred from any relief under plans to raise money for road construction, as the small head-rents payable to the landlord were inadequate security for loans, as the chief rents were payable to a widow up to 1852, under the terms of a settlement.

'Black '47' has well merited its soubriquet. In January of that year, one-third of those listed as destitute were not yet on the public works rolls. At this time, many seeking relief were too feeble to work and 'the idleness of the idle could no longer be distinguished from the feebleness of the weak and infirm'. At the end of the month, the government announced the end of the public works, which was really an admission that this system of providing relief had been largely a failure. Designed to avoid inefficiency, waste and extravagance, it was, in fact, the most costly method of providing relief during the course of the Famine. Also on 30 January, the *Illustrated London News*, perhaps horrified by reports of mass deaths and perhaps as a protest at the inaction of politicians influenced by Whig ideology, who did not close the ports, stated that as 'Ireland had already suffered from years of misgovernment, they should now provide more rather than less intervention, on the ground that neglect, carelessness, laissez-faire did not make a cheap system of government'.

The government announced that famine relief would be transferred to the Poor Law in the autumn of the year. To facilitate the change-over, the Soup Kitchen Act (Burgoyne's Act) was passed in February 1847, as a temporary measure to supply food to some categories of the destitute in a horrible system of outdoor relief; women, recently widowed, whose only income derived from the public works, were cut off; and several, especially those with children, either begged or entered workhouses.

In the same months, the Navigation Acts were finally suspended and all duties on foreign corn suspended; these actions were too little, too late, for many people; however, some people who still had resources benefitted from the falling price of food. In the meantime, committees appointed to distribute food began to operate. Three categories were entitled to gratuitous relief – destitute unemployed labourers, the infirm and destitute landholders. Working labourers were prohibited from getting free food. If their wages were unable to feed their families, they were allowed only to purchase food, paying at least cost price. Despite the fact that many wages were inadequate to provide food for families, the Relief Commissioners absolutely forbade gratuitous assistance, which would supplement inadequate wages. Ironically, unemployed labourers often obtained more food, free of charge, than working labourers who were compelled to work for it. As a result, many labourers left their employers to qualify for gratuitous aid. This system caused much hardship to women and children.

Much public debate centred on whether food should be distributed cooked or uncooked. Many local committees gave out uncooked food for a time, despite the disapproval of the Relief Commissioners, as it was less troublesome than providing cooked food. Many of the poor preferred this system at first, until they realised that several people not truly in want were obtaining food, which was sold for exorbitant prices elsewhere. (There were some winners in the dire conditions of the Great Famine.) Finally, the distribution of cooked food, which was deemed a suitable test of destitution, was accepted as the norm. Women were compelled to bring the whole family to the soup kitchen daily; they were forced to stand in long lines, perhaps after having travelled long distances in bad weather. Women were annoyed when they realised that their rations were tampered with in the interests of economy. The size of the daily ration was specified as one pound of meal or flour or any grain, or one pound of biscuit or one-and-a-half pounds of bread. In practice, the raw ration consisted of two-thirds Indian meal and one-third rice (when obtainable); when cooked with water this mixture swelled to five pounds.

The Soup Kitchen Scheme, whatever its defects, proved the best means of relieving hunger between 1846 and 1851. For those who obtained food under this scheme, starvation and fever were generally averted. Many families bemoaned the suppression of the scheme in September 1847 and the enforcement of the Poor Law Acts of the same year, under which the government granted loans for improvements to Irish landlords, and passed the Encumbered Estates Act (including the infamous Gregory clause) to clear Ireland of bankrupt landlords. The Poor Law of June 1847 provided that the 'impotent poor', that is, the aged, sick orphans, the infirm, widows with two or more legitimate children, were to be relieved in or out of the workhouses, according to the decision of the local Board of Guardians. The unemployed able-bodied, if destitute, were entitled to relief only within the work-houses; they might receive assistance outside only if the workhouse was overcrowded or disease-ridden. In such cases, they might receive outdoor relief for a maximum period of two months, but only in the form of food for those willing to break stones, which was another test of destitution. Some women in Eyrecourt were forced to do such work to obtain relief.

No one occupying more than a quarter acre of land would be relieved out of the Poor Rates (the Gregory clause). This law aimed to assist landlords to clear their estates of poor tenants, who were paying little or no rent; they could only get relief for themselves and their families by giving up their holdings. Several families starved to death rather than surrender their miserable holdings, some in an attempt to retain their holdings, others lest they miss an opportunity of landlord-assisted emigration; in general, though, the law achieved its main aim.

The dreadful conditions in the workhouses in early 1847 forced the authorities to carry out several improvements, such as the expansion of workhouse accommodation, both permanent and temporary (the auxiliary workhouses) the granting of outdoor relief to the able-bodied poor, the construction of separate fever hospitals and extra dispensaries. Yet, the workhouses remained persistently overcrowded, because of determined efforts of local boards of guardians to avoid giving outdoor relief to the able-bodied poor, or to restrict such assistance as much as possible. In Mayo and Galway, guardians feared that if they abandoned the workhouse test, they would be overwhelmed by people seeking outdoor relief. To make sure of having sufficient workhouse places to test the destitution of able-bodied applicants for assistance, many guardians transferred the qualified impotent poor who were not seriously ill to the outdoor relief rolls; in fact, they provided outdoor relief to certain groups of people technically not entitled to such assistance, including widows with one dependant child, childless widows over 60, women deserted by their husbands before June 1847 and orphans whose relatives or friends were willing to shelter them. Relief officials felt it necessary to increase workhouse accommodation to restrain the demands for outdoor relief; they well understood that the poor hated the workhouse regimen and would only enter them as a last resort. However, once the workhouses filled in February and March 1848, the Poor Law Commissioners sanctioned outdoor relief for the destitute able-bodied poor, as well as for some classes of women and children who, strictly speaking, did not qualify for such assistance. The Commissioners actually advised Boards of Guardians to set up soup kitchens once again in 1848. Some did; but, in this year, many people did not collect cooked food because of exceptionally harsh weather. To assist the poor, the Vice-Guardians of the Clifden Union placed boilers four miles apart to limit the travel of the Union poor to a maximum of two miles coming for soup and two miles returning home; this arrangement was an exception to the general rule.

Of interest is the treatment of those affected by the Gregory clause; while the Poor Law Commissioners adhered to the strict letter of the law against relieving the actual occupiers of more than a quarter acre, the Gregory clause was eventually relaxed for their wives and children, who had been refused all assistance for about a year. In late May 1848, on legal advice, the Commissioners

circularised all Boards of Guardians stating that the destitute
dependants of 'obstinate' smallholders were now eligible for assistance in the workhouse, or outside, if the workhouse was full.
However, the Guardians were cautioned against giving assistance
'indiscriminately' to the dependants of persons occupying more
than a quarter acre of land. This caution was necessary as local
Guardians received very many applications for assistance, many
bogus, from women who stated that they were deserted wives,
and from children who stated that they were orphans or deserted
by their parents. Many spouses and parents were unwilling either
to enter the workhouses or break stones out-of-doors to provide
relief for their families. One should not be surprised by this
behaviour. *The Times* of 21 June 1849, reporting on the Tuam
and Ballinasloe Unions, stated that the peasantry had 'famine
unmistakably marked on their brows'. Homelessness had become
a major problem because of the operation of the Gregory clause;
landlords in Connacht as well as Munster 'abused the quarter-
acre clause to turn bankrupt smallholders out of possession *en
masse*. There was a rage for clearances'. Many bankrupt estates
were sold, but poor tenants found that new owners frequently
continued the eviction policies of the previous owners. These
included John Gerrard at Mountbellew, Francis Twinnings at
Cleggan and James Thorngate on the Castlefrench estate in
County Galway.

Despite the intervention of the government to assist the poorest
unions through two rates-in-aid, levied on all rateable property
in Ireland, the Poor Law Guardians were distressed in many
Unions, including Clifden, Tuam and Gort as these taxes were
almost impossible to collect. Many Unions now attempted to
reduce their costs by encouraging potential long-term inmates,
including young orphans and young girls, to emigrate. However,
the pattern visible during the Famine prevailed throughout the
century, when distressed women resorted to the workhouses. It is
more difficult to quantify the assistance granted by individuals
and organisations during times of distress. Among the more
effective organisations were the Society of Friends (Quakers),

who realised at the end of 1846 that the public works were failing
to contain starvation and disease. They became directly involved
and introduced a system of distributing cheap food directly to the
starving poor, as a short-term measure, to end in the autumn of
1847, when the new poor law system would begin to function.
The Society of Friends also realised, from the reports of officers,
such as Forster (who gives his name to a street and park in Galway
City) that people's clothing was inadequate. They procured supplies of clothing overseas, particularly in the USA. This mode of
relief was not intended to interfere with the workings of the Poor
Law; it tended to lessen pauperism as it provided people who
were seeking work with suitable clothing. As many clothes distributed as relief were pawned, it was suggested that these coarse
woollen and cotton garments should be stamped, to make them
unacceptable to pawnbrokers as pledges.

The British Relief Association, which provided much help for
women and children during the Famine, sought the help of the
Poor Law Commissioners in 1848 to ensure that crops were
planted, thus avoiding a repetition of the poor harvest of the
previous autumn. In 1848, the Association made relief to the
children contingent on their parents working on the land, thus
forcing a return to the normal pattern of rural life. This proved a
blessing as by the summer of that year, the funds of the Association
were almost exhausted and they were forced to cut the rations
which they gave to school pupils. The people of Galway were
very fortunate because various religious groups co-operated to
provide assistance; members of all-male religious orders were
active officials on various relief committees. The main soup kitchen
in Galway city was efficiently run by a Protestant clergyman,
with assistance from various priests. The Sisters of Mercy fed
between 500 and 600 women and children, mainly children,
daily. The Presentation Sisters had taken over the Female and
Orphan Asylum Charity School, where before the famine 160 poor
children were fed, lodged and clothed. The *Galway Vindicator* of
3 March 1847 stated that an average of 354 children were fed daily
in the Presentation Convent from 21 to 28 February inclusive. The

Dominicans in the Claddagh founded three schools, on 11 August 1847; in the industrial department of the Piscatorial School, poor girls were taught spinning and enabled by their efforts to get food and clothing. The Dominicans, who also gave food directly to the destitute, stressed the importance of permanent relief in the form of education. Fr Folan of the Claddagh (Dominican) community stated, when seeking educational funds, that:

> If the people had been better educated, they would not have suffered all the misery that they did during the last few years, for an educated people would not endure poverty and destitution, if there were any remedy for them within reach.

The Augustinians raised much-needed cash by their annual charity sermons for the support of the Christian Doctrine Society, which in 1849 clothed 800 destitute girls. Religious orders did not work in isolation: in October 1848, a charity sermon in the Dominican Church raised £20 for the support of the female children of the Presentation Convent School. During a Vincentian mission in Galway in 1852, the noted preacher, Fr Rinolfi, raised funds for the Dominicans and the Augustinian Christian Doctrine Society. The Franciscans subscribed to the efforts of the other orders and organisations to procure famine relief as well as providing spiritual help for the destitute. In the Tuam area, the Presentation Sisters were compelled to abandon formal education and substitute social services during the years 1847 and 1848.

Members of all religious organisations worked actively to obtain relief from abroad, including £24,000 from Calcutta. Sr. Mary de Pazzi, a Galway Presentation Sister and a member of the O'Donnel family of Newport, County Mayo, wrote letters to a cousin, Count Maurice O'Donnel of Austria, appealing for relief to enable the Sisters to continue giving one meal per day to poor afflicted children; this good sister received help from Rome, Yorkshire, New York and Chicago. Such attempts by Religious Orders to aid the poor continued for much of the century. Of great interest is data relating to the Mercy Convent, Clifden, founded in 1853. Aside from providing schools, the nuns assisted the poor. A letter from them to the *Victorian* in August 1862 led to the foundation of the Irish Relief Committee in Melbourne. The Sisters may have decided to write to Melbourne, because Mr Michael J. Page-Hannify, a native of Clifden, was a Justice of the Peace there. The *Galway Vindicator* noted on 26 November 1862 that the Mansion House Relief Committee had already received £500 from this committee and that a further £2,000 was on its way from Melbourne. Later, the *Galway Vindicator* of 20 May 1863 reported that the Irish Relief Committee had adopted a recommendation to expend £2,000 to supply free passages to 100 industrious men and eligible women, as they believed that assisted emigration was the most permanent and effective mode of relief:

> They will be able soon after their arrival to remit to their friends and distressed districts more than the cost of their passages . . . who may in turn obtain the passages of others under the Assisted Emigration Scheme.

Those travelling were to be transported on a first-class ship, and a small sum of money was also set apart for the outfit of each person at the port of Galway. The efforts of this committee did much to give a new start in life to many people from one of the country's most distressed districts. These people brought with them memories of tragedy so graphically described by some contemporaries. In January 1847, Forster found both potatoes and turnips gone and desperation everywhere in Ballinahinch barony; distraught poor people sought relief in towns, such as Clifden and in Galway city. In March 1847, Jonathan Pim and James Perry on a visit to Clifden noted people dying in the streets, the wasted pinched faces of the living, extreme distress aggravated by the outbreak of dysentery and the collapse of the overburdened Poor Law Union.

Details of suffering are horrifying: a woman's corpse was partly eaten by dogs in Clifden, a pauper would have been buried without even a shroud, had not a passing gentleman paid for a coffin. In autumn, there were 140 bodies scattered on the highway near Clifden awaiting burial. Whole families died of fever, when 'the last survivor earthed up the door of the cabin to prevent the ingress of pigs and dogs and laid himself/herself to die in this fearful vault'. In November 1847, three-quarters of the town's population were suffering from typhus and related fevers, and, to aggravate the general misery, the land in the area had not been cultivated the previous year.

People from distressed rural areas, including boat-loads from Connemara, arrived in Galway city, frequently on the point of death; their corpses lay by hedges and ditches with nobody to bury them. The *Galway Vindicator* of 13 March 1847 carried harrowing accounts, such as that of Celia Griffin, for whom assistance simply came too late. She was but one of many. Events in the city reveal the effects of the Famine on all ranks of society, with small tradesmen begging for soup and clergy and landlords receiving neither dues nor rent. Forster stated, however, that famine mortality would have been greater in any other country; many lives had been prolonged, perhaps saved, by the long apprenticeship to want in which the Irish peasant had been trained and by the loving, touching charity which prompted him to share his scanty meal with his starving neighbour. He was particularly impressed by one such example in Claddagh. Elsewhere, people were driven to desperation in their search for food. In the terrible winter of 1847, horses, asses, snails, frogs, crows and hedgehogs baked in clay were consumed. Starving people ate the carcasses of diseased cattle, dogs and dead horses, even in the winter of 1848–9, when Trevelyan had stated that the famine was at an end, but principally they ate wild herbs, nettle tops, wild mustard and water cresses. It is not surprising that deaths in County Galway increased from 12,582 in 1848 to 15,939 in 1849; in some places, corpses had grasses in their mouths. Some instances of cannibalism occurred; the *Freeman's Journal* in April 1848 reported that in County Galway a mother had eaten part of her dead son's body.

To the misery of starvation was added the scourge of fever, which added considerably to the difficulties of women's lives. In normal times, when women became ill, help was freely available, if the ailment was non-contagious.

If women contracted fever, 'the plague of Ireland', little help was available. The sick person was put into a hut or the family left the house; nourishment was left at the door and the patient had to crawl out and take it in. A woman might tend her sick children and husband suffering from fever, but no other relative would. While dispensaries had become more common since 1824, not everybody trusted them; in Clifden the number of patients treated diminished after 1830 as sick people feared both the doctors and medicine 'to whom (ironically) the peasantry attributed the propagation of cholera'. This attitude boded ill for the period, when Famine fever, once called road fever and later ship fever, when it afflicted ships' passengers, was prevalent. Road fever was a combination of dysentery and typhus (*an Fiabhras Dubh*) which affected mainly the elderly. Much illness was caused by bad, contaminated food, such as bad shellfish in Oranmore. Most people did not know that several diseases were lice-borne; one who did was Mr St George of Headford, who condemned beggars with attendant vermin for spreading typhus fever, itch and scrofula. A Mr Cassidy spoke of children's diseases, such as smallpox, measles and whooping cough being spread in towns and villages by beggars.

One did not need to be lice-infested to contract these diseases: lice excrement, dried to a light dust could infect even healthy people, when wind-blown. Sadly, people who fled disease-ridden Ireland actually carried fever with them on coffin-ships; the *Midas*, which left Galway in May 1847 destined for St John's, New Brunswick, lost one tenth of its passengers at sea. (Famine fever inspired terror in the countries to which Irish famine refugees fled and was one of the factors which led to anti-Irish prejudice.) Children also suffered from ophalemia, blindness induced by starvation; scurvy, hitherto unknown, made an appearance in Ireland and was directly linked to potato failures. Scurvy was known as *cos dubh* or black leg, as its victims' legs turned black; it also caused people's teeth to fall out. Disease spread rapidly among people with low resistance, who lived in horrific living conditions; dung-heaps were frequently sited near the front doors of cabins while Galway city had just two sewers at this time.

Sadly, some of the food which people now began to use as a substitute for the potato led to disease; starvation compelled many people to use edible sea weeds and shellfish for the first time. Shore food was only used by many of the destitute before the Famine. 'Seachain tigh an tabhairne nó is bairnigh is beatha duit' (Beware of the public house – avoid it – or you will be forced to eat limpets) was advice frequently given to the young. It was women's work to collect such food. Many women were not aware that certain shellfish must be boiled and are fatal if eaten raw after a long fast; bad shellfish caused illness and death. Coastal dwellers knew that *dilisk* eaten cold is dangerous and that *dulamán* or channelled wrack is not eaten until after the first severe frost. Many women thought they were cursed as substitutes for the potato also caused disease and death. The lack of food and the spread of disease forced some people to enter the decimating workhouses, which were termed 'human swineries' by Carlyle. Ironically, fever raged in them, caused, in part, by overcrowding. People who might have received medical treatment in the infirmaries of workhouses, sometimes delayed seeking admission until their illness was too far advanced. Others, such as the dysentery victims in County Galway in November 1840 had to travel long distances in inclement weather to enter the workhouses. The lack of hygiene in some workhouses, such as Tuam and Oughterard, was also a powerful factor in the spread of disease. However, as the Famine raged, people's unwillingness to enter workhouses largely disappeared.

Another reaction to starvation and famine was to emigrate. Women travelled considerable distances to pawn clothing, nets and fishing tackle from areas such as Innisboffin in 1848, to raise cash to purchase food or to emigrate. Traditional attitudes towards emigration changed dramatically; the Crown estates of Boughill and Ivrilloughter (Ahascragh) provided assisted passages to Canada for 243 of their tenants, which included many women and children. These tenants had refused assisted passages in 1836 but in 1846, when reduced to eating nettles and diseased potatoes, they begged to be sent to America. While heavy emigration to America had begun after 1822, there was a reluctance to split families up to the time of the Great Famine, a reluctance which disappeared when the emigration of one member might save the rest from death at home. The pattern of chain migration became acceptable in the desperate circumstances of the time.

At home, traditional family bonds broke; Captain Holland of Galway Workhouse referred to several cases who were considered for admission where husbands had left their wives and wives their husbands in their cabins to perish of fever, while they sought an asylum in the workhouse, thus showing the miserable state of feeling to which these unfortunate people had been reduced 'from want of the common necessities of life'. Grown children threw parents out on the roads and mothers even withheld food from their children. Women, in particular, depended on the workhouses. The records of St Nicholas' parish in Galway, which included a male workhouse, an auxiliary workhouse, gaol, infirmary and fever hospital, revealed that females outnumbered male inmates in both 1841 and 1851. There was no woman in the auxiliary workhouse of this parish in 1841, but there were 910 there ten years later.

Marriage rates which had begun to decline after the famine of 1822 fell dramatically after the Great Famine. Women now regarded early marriage as reckless, and began to consider non-marriage as a viable option, particularly overseas. Many were haunted by the prospects of the poorhouse, the pauper's grave and a life of dependence and of poverty, if they remained in Ireland; their fears were well founded. They also realised that the particular problem in Ireland during the Famine was one of overpopulation and consequent destitution, as much as food shortages; they were painfully aware that there was plenty of food in Ireland, if they had the money to buy it; thus, money wages as a symbol of security, became of paramount importance to them. Those who could sought secure employment both at home and abroad, often postponing or avoiding marriage to ensure this security. It is easy to understand the desire of many Irish women to emigrate, particularly to America, which represented opportunities for money wages and advancement, unavailable at home. The final memory of many women as they boarded the emigrant ship was of

> entire villages being levelled to the ground, miles of country lying idle and unproductive without the face of a human being on it. The hare had made his form on the hearth, and the lapwing wheeled over the ruined cabin.

As reports of continuing destitution reached these exiles, it must have seemed to many of them as if conditions would never improve, particularly in later crises, such as the winter of 1879–80, when once again the duchess of Marlborough spoke of

> a spirit of harmony and conciliation influencing those who are working under the resident gentlemen, Protestant clergymen and Catholic priests who appear to have but one object in view – namely the mitigating of the calamity, which has afflicted parts of Ireland, relieving distress wherever it exists.

The areas of continuing distress were also the areas of extreme distress during the Great Famine; such distress became the focus of relief work for mainly middle-class women, of all religious denominations. Their work was mainly aimed at destitute women and children, following the accepted social norms of the time. Help was dispensed to the 'deserving poor' – men and women who, although willing to work, were unable to do so, 'either through illness or lack of opportunity'. In rural areas, wives, daughters and sisters of landowners helped to alleviate distress. Several women tried to relieve poverty by creating employment among the poor, including the 'genteel poor'. Much Catholic aid was administered by nuns, who provided 'the most intensive network of charitable organisations and societies' until the end of the century. The work of nuns, however, excluded lay Catholic women, many of whom were not as well placed to administer relief.

There were far more lay women belonging to other religious denominations involved in philanthropy. The charitable societies inspired by religious motives played a specific role in the lives of poor women 'who used them to tide them over the lean periods'.

The Victorian idea of respectability, especially sexual respectability, permeated work for the relief of distress. In the workhouses, which were refuges for distressed women throughout the century, great efforts were made to separate 'respectable' women from the 'unrespectable'. Those who did not wish to enter the workhouses were frequently dependent on the efforts of philanthropic women or clergy. Public subscriptions continued to be collected for various almshouses, such as the Widows and Orphans Refuge in College Road in Galway. Special efforts were made for destitute newly-orphaned children. Indeed, in the grim winter of 1879–80, only the great outpouring of private charity and the funds provided by the Duchess of Marlborough's Committee and the Mansion House Committee prevented a disaster as great as the Great Famine. The ensuing distress led to the foundation of the Land League, which also gave relief, although it did not co-operate with other relief committees. In various subsistence crises, government intervention continued. Thus, in 1880–1, Dublin Castle financed large imports of rice and maize from America and used the Army Commissariat structure to reduce regional scarcities. They were assisted by women who were involved in local distribution networks. Relief of distress was thus a major occupation of women in nineteenth-century Ireland, whether as recipients or providers. There was great need for their services:

> Whether it was house visitations, instituting an orphanage or school, working in prisons, refuges or workhouses, philanthropy became the principal, if largely unpaid, occupation of a great number of middle-class Irishwomen in the nineteenth century.

22: Augusta Crofton at Clonbrock House, May 1866

23: A woman in lace cap and plaid shawl at Clonbrock House

24: Drawingroom, Clonbrock House

25: Clonbrock House

MIGRATION AND EMIGRATION

Migration and emigration both played a major part in determining the pattern of population change throughout the nineteenth century. In Ireland, the character of both changed quite considerably during the course of the century. For instance, for much of the earlier part of the century, there were no significant numbers of female migratory workers, unlike Ireland in the post-Famine period.

What is migration? To be worthy of the name it must involve a significant number of people; it must be sustained (not temporary or casual) and it must include a distinct social transition involving a change of status or a changed relationship to the social as well as the physical environment. Temporary migration implies that the place of permanent residence is maintained, while the migrant is away for a period of work in another country or another part of the country on a regular or seasonal basis, such as transhumance or harvest migration. There is much evidence of temporary migration in its various aspects, in county Galway during the period under study; some of it was very localised, such as that of Aran fishermen coming to the mainland to fish. Migration was largely a rural phenomenon; few left the towns and city, which in turn, attracted some migrants. Galway City was regarded as 'the refugium peccatorum (refuge of sinners or last refuge) of all outcasts' in its appeal for beggars and migrant workers. This was atypical as there was little scope for migration to towns because there was little town growth, either in size, work opportunities or population.

It was only in the 1880s that it was really possible to examine the geographical spread of migration, as little relevant data had been collected in earlier years. In 1881, however, the official figures confirmed a pattern that was already in evidence in 1834.

Seasonal migration in different poor law unions per 1,000 population	
Union of Glenamaddy	39.5
Union of Tuam	28.5
Union of Mountbellew	22.5

Source: P.P. 1881 (lxciii) p. 38

These figures are consistent with the national pattern where up to the 1890s migration was chiefly confined to interior regional areas, where there were large farms and few chances of employment. The mobility of seasonal workers from these areas increased due to the development of the railway networks of the 1840s and 1850s. The west of the county did not have railways for much of the period and migration became more important in this district after the Famine than earlier in the century.

Within the areas where migration predominated, there were large variations between one parish and another. In some parishes, such as Donamon and Ballymacward, only single men migrated for the harvest; in Castleblakeney, married men departed, and both single and married men migrated from Kilglass and Monivea.

Women employed a variety of coping strategies to deal with migration. In general, it was customary for wives and children to remain in Ireland. Many, particularly of the cottier class, begged in the more opulent counties, particularly if the summer was bad, the potato crop failed and no help was forthcoming from family or friends. If at all possible, women tried to stay in their own homes. In order to do so, some existed on one scant meal daily; 'they lived by the potato'. Some men obtained provisions for their wives and families, often at a rate of 30–35% interest for the time absent, to be repaid on their return home from migratory labour. Women, in the absence of their menfolk, tended crops either on their own behalf or for landlords and did heavy work, such as footing turf.

Inevitably, some were less able to cope than others. These resorted, in several cases, to the workhouses, as a temporary measure, pretending to be deserted wives. In the Relief Extension

Act of 1847, it was stated that 'people going from one Union to another seeking relief, abandoning families and leaving them to become a burden on the state were liable to be charged with vagrancy'. This legislation was an attempt to eradicate a key subsistence strategy in the lives of cottiers and the poorest labourers – the absence of the man from the family for part of the year. That women would resort to such a strategy is understandable, particularly when early summer, with its regular food shortages, was marked by a wave of migrants 'imposed on a permanent stream of beggars who moved through the country at all times of the year'. Among these migrants were several who had been evicted; others became involved in short-distance migration for a time after evictions, before emigrating or, in some cases, being reinstated as tenants on worse terms.

Migration played a 'crucial part in the search for subsistence'. Up to 1860, it was estimated that the income from seasonal harvest work amounted to £10 – more than one third of the budget of many families in the West of Ireland – and was often used to pay the rent. However, it has been estimated that the amount earned by the harvesters dwindled steadily from £10–£15 in the 1860s to sums from £8–£10 during the 1890s. This was mainly the result of a fall in grain prices from 1879 because of cheap American grain imports into Britain and the effects of harvesting machinery, such as horse-drawn reapers and steam threshing machines (introduced in the 1840s) on the demand for harvest labourers. This was in direct contrast with events in the earlier part of the century, when a growing demand for migratory labour in England coincided with increasing unemployment in Ireland. At that period, a new system had evolved in England, which involved two principal figures, the large farmer and the hired labourer. As a reaction to the new development, many seasonal harvesters turned to permanent urban migration, in cities such as York, by the latter half of the century. However, seasonal migration played a part in maintaining pre-Famine conditions in much of the West, until the last years of the century.

The hardship imposed on women and children by migration has been under-rated. However, it is fair to say that 'both before and after the mid-century famine crisis, the contribution by the women in allowing the family to hold on to the family plot was at least equal, if not more important, than the part played by the men'. Much of this was achieved by women and families tending to agricultural tasks etc. in the absence of their menfolk.

Not many women migrants left Ireland until the post-Famine period. When they did, it was often by a process called 'stepwise migration' – first to England and then to the USA, which shows that migration and emigration overlapped. Peaks in emigration corresponded with failures of the potato crop:

Failure of potatoes	*Peak in emigration*
1829–30	1830–32
1832–34	1834
1836	1836–37
1839	1841–42

From the time of the Great Famine, more women than men emigrated. Very many emigrants from Galway emigrated through the port of Dublin, although ships sailed regularly from Galway to the USA. This suggests that stepwise migration was an integral part of the pattern of emigration and many migrants later emigrated to the USA through ports such as Liverpool and Glasgow.

As shown on the following table, between May 1851 and December 1855, 19,199 females and males left Galway. The peak year was 1852, when 10,222 males and females left the county.

It is widely held that most of those who emigrated were unskilled and uneducated; however, figures for Galway reveal that many of the women who left trained as dressmakers and seamstresses. Between May 1851 and December 1855, a total of 3,742 dressmakers and 3,909 seamstresses, left, with 1,148 leaving

Year	Galway		Belfast		Drogheda		Dublin		Limerick		Derry & Moyville		Cork	
	M	F	M	F	M	F	M	F	M	F	M	F	M	F
1851	777	870	7				2964	2969	12	19	43	35	4	
1852	320	355	8	6	6		4633	4694	21	20	64	83		
1853	215	261	12	6			4049	3986	16	68	125	113	5	2
1854	283	490					3297	3305			49	49		
1855	77	11					1237	1530	7	4	84	76		

Emigration from Galway Town and County through various ports to overseas destinations, including England, Scotland, Wales and America

Sources: 1851 Census Table XXXV, showing the number of emigrants who left each county in Ireland from 1 May 1851 to 31 December 1855, stating it to be their intention not to return, compiled from accounts taken at several Irish ports. 1852: Table X, Appendix to General Report; 1853: Table XI. 1854: Table XII. 1855: Table XIII

in 1852, 700 in 1851 and 825 in 1854. These figures reflect unemployment at home and the attraction of life overseas.

Many of these women had been employed in the houses of large landlords, several of whom were ruined by the Great Famine and its aftermath with their estates sold in the Encumbered Estates Court.

Many women and their families emigrated through assisted emigration schemes, such as that at Irvilloughter. The earlier inhibition towards emigration 'withered like the potato stalks on a ruined landscape'. For both Irish men and women, emigration became an expected episode in the life cycle. Many single women emigrated, particularly if they had little chance of marriage, or of carving a niche for themselves in some worthwhile employment; some had little to take with them other than their hopes. For many Irish women, as well as those over much of rural Western Europe, the choice was not between rural unemployment or urban work as a domestic servant, but rather a choice between the subordinate role of an unpaid helper in her own family or the freedom and independence which a paying job in a distant city promised. Female emigrants from Ireland had little chance of finding native-born husbands or non-menial employment, but even the humblest husband or job abroad was better than no husband and no job at home. Emigrant women saw themselves largely as independent economic agents, many of them attending evening schools to better prepare themselves for life overseas. Indeed, the Famine and post-famine emigration was a catalyst of change in social attitudes towards the role of women in Irish life, though change was to come very slowly. Several of those who emigrated were no longer content to accept the 'subject, subsidiary and restricted role of women' in Ireland and through their remittances fuelled further emigration, particularly along the female line. It was gradually accepted that many of the more enterprising men and women emigrated and a sense of failure sometimes attached to those who remained behind. This occurred at a time when poverty was reduced gradually by means of net migration, reduced marriage and reproductive rates – described by one historian as 'the multi-component system that is human adaptation to ecological stress'.

Both migration and emigration were to have lasting effects on Irish people, psychologically damaged by the Famine. In many ways, Irish society became warped and was characterised by 'an abiding sense of fatalism', a fatalism which may have been a potent factor in the failure of Irish people to make the best use of the country's resources or capitalise upon its opportunities. A peculiar cumulative restlessness was ascribed to people accustomed

26: Traditional housing at Dogfish Lane in the Claddagh,
beside the Claddagh Church

to migration from childhood and was a major factor in both
migration and emigration, particularly when linked with an
enduring illusion that the next town or country would, after all,
be paved with gold. Such an attitude is succinctly expressed in
Gaelic as 'Is glas iad na cnoic i bhfad i gcéin' (Far away hills are
green) and it was often accompanied by a type of double nostalgia,
where Irish emigrants might lament their exile, while potential
emigrants in Ireland looked longingly towards foreign shores.

WOMEN AND CRIME

Women of the period were law-abiding. Women accounted for
about 40% of criminal offences, which were generally divided
into three broad categories:

1 offences against property;

2 offences against the person;

3 offences against behaviour, which mainly consisted of
drunkenness, disorderly behaviour, vagrancy and prostitution.

Most offences, arrests and convictions for both men and women
were in the third category. In 1840, for example, three-quarters
of the arrests (men and women), were in this category.

The rights of property owners were regarded as sacred, and
crimes against property were treated quite harshly by the judiciary.
In spite of this, several women were involved in theft, often for
the necessities of life, such as fuel, clothing, food and less frequently cash, when in great want. Food was usually stolen when
food prices became inflated in times of near-famine. Women
were involved in food riots involving theft of 'flour, barley and
oatmeal' during the Famine. Theft or injury to fowl figured
prominently in the petty sessions. Other forms of theft were less
obvious, such as the use of 'short measure' used by women in the
markets. A typical case was that of Bridget Connor, who was fined
4s. at Galway assizes in 1841 for having two small pint measures in
her possession, which did not hold more than three noggins (a
quarter pint) each, which she used when selling buttermilk.

Fuel was both scarce and expensive in many areas. In some
districts, bogs were effectively closed against the poor who could
not afford to pay rent of 6s. to 8s. per perch. This meant that
bushes and branches were cut down for fuel. When shortages
occurred, even children were 'sent out to steal fuel'. Lack of fuel
also impinged greatly on the lives of the town poor, where it was
often stolen. Cash was sometimes stolen, but less frequently than
other items for several reasons: there was little cash in circulation
in the early part of the century and sudden affluence or increased
spending would immediately arouse the suspicion of the police,
begrudging neighbours or even family members. In fact, many of
the women accused of stealing money were convicted of the
charge.

The actions of some landlords, both men and women, provoked crime against both property and the person. Public feeling ran very high in Galway, where between 1852 and 1864, civil bill ejectments, affecting 735 defendants, were registered for County Galway, while Mayo registered 24 ejectments for the same period. A notorious case involving a female landlord in County Galway was that of Mrs Gerrard, who ordered the eviction of 300 villagers from Ballinglass in 1846 in an attempt to change agricultural holdings to grazing land. These tenants were not in arrears, and had actually reclaimed 400 acres of bog, adding value to the land. This episode, which was the subject of a special enquiry by Lord Londonderry, led to outrages; as starvation spread among the evicted tenants, a group of 100 women, with their children, stole about two tons of meal from government supplies being transported to Cork. Women were also accused of arson and incendiarism, conviction for which might lead to transportation. Female arrests under this category dropped significantly as the century wore on, although the worst years of distress showed a very high number of arrests.

In general, nearly four times as many women were charged with offences, rarely serious, against the person. In this category, in 1840, the main charges against women were for assaults which comprised 83.3% of arrests, while several were charged with obstructing the police in the course of their duty. Charges for assault increased throughout the century. Crimes against the person at times involved relatively minor attacks on neighbours, arising from seemingly trivial incidents, caused by poverty, overcrowding and disease. The Irish adage that 'Is fearr socrú dá olcas ná dlí dá fheabhas' (The worst settlement is better than the best law) rarely applied in these cases; one magistrate commented that 'they are prone to litigation and value their time but little; they will sometimes summon for the trespass of a hen'.

More serious crimes against the person involved murder, manslaughter, infanticide and serious assaults; many of these crimes being alcohol-related. At Galway Town criminal assizes in 1852 Catherine Heavy was convicted of attempted murder and sentenced to 15 years transportation; she was caught red-handed in her attempt. Some murder attempts, however, reveal ingenuity as to the means employed. Bridget Ruane attempted unsuccessfully to murder her newly-wed husband by adding to his porridge sublimate of lead, bought in Tuam 'for a sore leg'.

As well as attempting to or actually murdering difficult or unwanted spouses, some women murdered children, both older children and infants. Many murdered children were illegitimate: Mary Conneely murdered her eight-year-old child by placing two stones around her neck and pushing her into Loughbeg, where her death was caused by a combination of strangulation and drowning. The child's mother was found guilty of wilful murder, but had absconded. Cases of infanticide were very difficult to prove: suspicions abounded but proof was elusive. Inquests into the deaths of these children make heart-rending reading, as they were either neglected, viciously murdered, or placed where they might be killed by animals. In Ardfry, an infant left on a manure heap at night was killed by a pig 'which lacerated and mangled the body'. This was not an isolated case. Some cases of infanticide revealed tragedies in mothers' lives; a married woman, whose husband had emigrated or migrated, might have a child by her lover. Such women were at pains to 'screen and secrete' (conceal) the births of their children. Several women were charged with concealing the birth of children, perhaps causing their deaths, but were generally acquitted for lack of evidence. The pressures on women who committed such crimes may have become unbearable because of the disapproval and lack of support of the wider society.

Some crimes were against both property and the person; these frequently occurred in rural districts where 'in contrast to those of Britain, the rural disturbances of Ireland were persistent, extensive, destructive and savage'. Many crimes had economic causes, others were linked to religion, such as crime relating to tithes. While major outbreaks of discontent had short-term causes, such as evictions and encroachment of pastoral farming on arable land, they also reflect the influence of deeper strains and pressures within Irish society, including conacre, a cause of much acrimony which more or less disappeared after the Famine, which resulted in the decimation of the cottier and landless labourer classes.

Offences against behaviour were crimes against respectability, some of which involved drunkenness. A drunken woman was regarded as a reprobate; there was a much greater tolerance of male drunkenness. Vagrancy was another offence of this type, punishable by harsh prison sentences. Vagrant women were regarded as having nuisance value. Others regarded as being reprobate were prostitutes, whose numbers increased alarmingly between 1863 and 1871, despite the passing of the Criminal Law Amendment Act (1865) which applied to them. They were the targets of police vigilance, who regarded them as 'fallen women', in a period when the so-called 'double standard' applied to sexual morality.

Another group of women and girls, whose behaviour was regarded as disreputable, were those who made false accusations of rape; some of these aroused religious animosity as well as outrage, particularly when clergy of other religious persuasions were accused, in an attempt to discredit them. In Galway, in 1835, a peasant pleaded that a Protestant minister had dishonoured his daughter and sued for damages and costs; suspecting that he was a 'straw man', the defending lawyer forced the accused to reveal, under cross-examination, that the money used to bring legal proceedings had been given to him by an enemy of the accused. Bankrupts were committed to prison during this period; not many women fell into this category as they found it difficult to obtain bank loans etc.

Women were also involved in attacks on the Revenue Police, especially when stills and apparatus for making poteen or illicit whiskey were seized. There would have been a certain grudging tolerance of this offence by society at large, as such seizures deprived some women of their livelihood.

Women were often victims of crime, which ranged from minor assault to murder. Some were domestic rows; in other cases, broken romances could lead to bitter recriminations, assaults, and, occasionally, murder. One such case was that of Bridget Barrett, of Roundstone, whose death was the subject of the first inquest held in Connemara, which led to charges of murder on the high seas against two men. The verdict was that on 10 September 1845 'the accused, James Mannion and Thomas Cosgriff, lured the deceased into a boat at Ruananule … murdered her'. The lurid details of this case received extensive publicity even in the midst of the Famine. The transportations register records that James Mannion, then aged 22, was convicted of murder on 5 August 1846. However, the death sentence was commuted to transportation for life. Mannion was one of many who died in prison while awaiting transportation.

Some women died as a result of horrific injuries, usually inflicted by stones or farmyard implements. Many brutal attacks on women were of a sexual nature; there is a body of evidence which reveals that many young girls were raped. For example, Patrick Clougherty was convicted of the brutal violation of a little girl ten years old 'on the clearest testimony'. A minority of women used rape charges to try to enforce marriage, which did not always take place. De Tocqueville, the noted French traveller, stated that such conduct 'proved a great coarseness of manners, but not impurity'.

The prevailing attitudes in society are reflected in sentencing policy: a double standard generally prevailed, not so much in the sentences handed down, but in the manner in which they were served. Crimes against property were severely dealt with by the courts. When large animals were stolen, both men and women received harsh sentences, which ranged from ten years' imprisonment to transportation for life for stealing cows.

Killing stolen animals was also punished by long terms of transportation, in many cases fifteen years. Proven larceny was treated harshly, especially if the accused had a bad reputation. The courts, however, showed admirable impartiality in evaluating evidence and recorded non-guilty verdicts in doubtful cases, and, occasionally awarded damages to those unjustly accused of theft. Those convicted of receiving stolen goods received harsh sentences. In 1843, Anne Quinn's two sons were involved in stealing £75 and were sentenced to ten years' transportation; their mother was sentenced to seven years transportation for receiving stolen goods and money. The profile of convict settlers in Australia reveals that the average age of Irish female convicts was 27, most of them single, only 34% of them having been married or widowed. Most of them were transported between 1830 and 1840, mainly for the crimes of animal stealing and arson.

Sentences imposed on women who committed violent crimes against the person were relatively lenient, when contrasted with sentences against property. The Transportation Register of 1841–2 reveals that:

1 Celia Donohue, aged 52, was transported for seven years for manslaughter.

2 Margaret Hynes, aged 64, was transported for seven years for larceny.

3 Eleanor Craddon was sentenced to fourteen years transportation for receiving stolen goods.

Crimes against the person and property frequently overlapped in charges of arson and incendiarism, convictions for which usually carried sentences of seven years' transportation. One woman, however, Honor Farrell, was sentenced to fifteen years transportation for incendiarism in Galway in 1850; the attack which led to this sentence was motivated by revenge, was meticulously planned and showed complete disregard for the occupants of her former employer's house.

When women were victims of crime, the legal penalties could range from very lenient to very harsh. A conviction for malicious assault on two women was punished by fourteen years' transportation in 1831. By contrast, in 1841 an assault on a female merited a fine of 2s. 6d and costs. There was little legal protection for women physically abused by their husbands, who might receive a derisory fine for such an attack; such an attitude may reflect the thinking current at that time, which said that a wife was the property of her husband. During the century, convictions for rape carried a death sentence, although imprisonment or transportation could be imposed. Female accusers and witnesses usually had their own lives examined for any deviant or undesirable behaviour (however remote from sexual misconduct) which might have proved a temptation to the men charged. Many rape cases were dismissed if purported victims did not give evidence against the accused; in some cases the parties involved married; in other cases, women were unwilling to face the rigours of the court. It is quite possible that some were bought off. Whatever the reason, the trials of many men accused of rape fell through, because of lack of evidence. On at least one occasion, a man convicted of rape, who was willing to marry his victim, found his wishes thwarted by factors beyond his control: one such was a soldier, found guilty of raping Catherine Bouchier, who was accompanied in court by his superior officer, who vouched for his character and stated:

> If marriage was solemnized between the parties, the man would escape (hanging): that without the consent of his officers, he could not be married and they would prefer him to be transported to bringing that woman into the Regiment.

'After that,' wrote the editor of the *Western Argus* (20 August 1820), 'who would be a soldier?'

Court sentences for crimes against behaviour reflected the preoccupation of society at large with the maintenance of public order, and were particularly harsh in some years, such as 1836 when there was a crackdown on such offences. Vagrancy was an offence, punishable by harsh prison sentences; for example, Elizabeth Monaghan in 1840 was sentenced to seven years imprisonment in the Galway courts. However, the convict reference books reveal that, in many instances, prisoners for this offence did not serve their full term. This usually happened when illness swept through the jails: thus, in 1848, all the Galway vagrants were discharged for this reason, and some prisoners, a proportion of whom were waiting to be transported, were released when fever was prevalent. The few women who were convicted of bankruptcy did not have a happy time in prison: an Inspector of Prisons reported on conditions for debtors in Galway Gaol; 'the female debtors are kept with female felons, vagrants, and those of the very worst character, of which they have rightly complained'.

While prisons consistently held more male than female prisoners, women were more likely than men to serve out their sentences, which were not always consistent. Women, who felt that they had been treated unduly harshly by the courts, could appeal to the Lord Lieutenant to have their sentences reduced. To obtain the mercy of the Lord Lieutenant, a woman needed to show that she did not commit any earlier offences, and her character had to be vouched for by respectable neighbours and the local parish priest or clergyman, together with the parson. Such appeals were generally unsuccessful. A rare exception was that of Mary Jones in 1845, who appealed against transportation and was imprisoned for an equal period in Ireland. Except in cases of murder and manslaughter, prisoners convicted for first offences would not be transported. Appeals against revenue offences were invariably refused. In 1852, for example, Mary Connor of Galway appealed against a conviction for selling illicit spirits. The magistrate stated that 'he could not interfere with the Excise'. One reads in amazement that while many men were reluctant to enter workhouses, they did not resent the jails as much; many actually hoped to be transported, others derived consolation from the fact that many harsh sentences for men were later reduced. The evidence available would suggest that this was a common practice in the case of convictions for crimes against women: a man sentenced to death for rape in 1841 served a mere two years in prison for this crime, as did a man who received mutton knowing it to have been stolen.

The plight of the mentally ill was little understood and many such people fell foul of the law, as suicide or attempted suicide was a criminal offence; in 1843 Mary Ann French, a native of

Loughrea, living in Galway in a state of abject misery, attempted to drown herself. She was discharged by the court, but was told that if found in Galway again, she would be indicted as a vagrant and transported! In the same court the difficulty of obtaining suitable medical treatment for the non-violent insane was highlighted. An unfortunate woman had hanged herself on the 'insane notion that she was the object of Satanic attack'. Attempts had been made to have her admitted to Ballinasloe Asylum. She could not be admitted until she became violent and dangerous, even though she herself wished to be admitted.

In spite of the Draconian conditions in prisons and other state institutions, they were sometimes used as a last-ditch survival strategy. The failure to obtain the necessities of life by lawful means caused many women to resort to crime and to look upon prison as a refuge, if admission to workhouses was refused. Anne Ward, in 1843, found guilty of petty theft, stated that she would re-offend, as she had been refused admission to the workhouse. This respectable woman, with three children, felt that 'the extremity of the Law was no more merciful than the Board of Guardians'. She deplored the necessity of such an action, but had no other choice to save her family and herself from starvation. After re-offending, an assistant barrister represented her case to the Poor Law Commissioners and she was finally admitted in May 1843.

Of interest are the figures for repeat offenders, which show that once a woman had more than five convictions, she became a hardened criminal. Judicial statistics for 1871 reveal that the number of women and girls who had more than ten convictions outnumbered male criminals with the same number of convictions by almost 3:1. It was felt that further legislation was required to deal with habitual criminals, especially women and it was suggested that the Reformatory System should be extended to this class of offender. It would have been very difficult for a woman to rehabilitate herself in the prevailing social climate. As so many of these women committed crimes against behaviour, they had considerable nuisance value for the police, who heartily disliked and disapproved of unruly women, some of whose behaviour in court did little to earn mercy: on at least one occasion, irate women physically attacked crown prosecutors. Some judges realised that there were contributing factors in many cases where crime was committed: this is reflected in the low conviction rates throughout the century, where the proportion of the acquitted and discharged was almost double that of England and Wales. Among the contributing factors in the case of women were unemployment, poor education and grim poverty. In 1840 about half of females convicted in Ireland were wholly uneducated. Of those committed for trial at assizes and quarter-sessions in 1862 and 1863, a disproportionate number were unable to read or write. In fact, the majority of female criminals lived economically marginal lives: in 1870 only 17% of convicted females were skilled workers and 10% had no occupation.

Many men and women were involved in crime, when they migrated or emigrated: in 1871, 22.6% of females in English prisons were of Irish birth, 10.9% in the case of men and boys. Although Scots in English jails were much fewer, women still outnumbered men by 2 to 1. The official explanation for this suggested that 'in both cases the difference arose from the migration of women of bad character from the poorer to the wealthier parts of the kingdom'. These figures may also reflect the difficulties faced by poorly educated women, resorting to a life of crime, when unable to provide for themselves by lawful employment.

One can only reflect in amazement on how few women became criminal, considering the poverty and hopelessness of many of their lives. Historians, such as Tom Hayden (1997), have argued that survivors of the Famine, both in Ireland and the USA, carried a legacy of shame, which they wished to excise by attaining respectability. Inherent in this desire was the desire to have 'a good name', clear of any imputation of crime. It also included zero tolerance towards those who offended against respectability. Others have argued that the Famine bred a profound distrust in its survivors, manifest as 'covert competitiveness which found poisonous expression in … incessant gossip and obsessive attention to the most minute indices of comparative status or respectability' on both sides of the Atlantic. The fear of becoming un-respectable, reinforced by the stifling force of public opinion, was a powerful motive in crime prevention, especially among girls and young women.

Epilogue

The subservient role played by many women in Irish society can be ascribed to several factors. From a legal point of view, the conquest of Ireland and subsequent plantations of the sixteenth and seventeenth centuries transformed the political, social and economic structure of Irish society. In this new society, women were totally without formal political rights, their property and inheritance rights, both within and outside marriage were now governed by English law; they played a subject and subsidiary role to the male for the most part. Lacking prescriptive status, the status of women in society was further reduced as a shift in the definition of work from being all contributions to the welfare and operation of society to a narrower definition based on a new idea of 'economic activity' which was introduced in the 1861 Census. In the second half of the century, women's non-wage labour counted for nought in official records, thus lowering status further. Oxley argues that adherence to notions of the market economy has led to the undervaluing of women's work performed in the unpaid or non-market sector.

The low status of women in Irish society is seen in the division of work along gender lines. A recurrent theme in historical accounts, travellers' tales and pictorial records during the century is the amount of heavy, physical work carried out by women in Ireland, particularly in rural areas. It would seem that the most arduous, unskilled physical work was undertaken by women: Wakefield in 1812, Dutton in 1824, Inglis in 1834 among others, all recorded their horror when they saw women used as load bearers before the Famine. In 1852, for instance, a Galway driver stated that 'the women carry loads as would do for horses. They do well in Americky [America].' Several men allotted the lightest work to themselves. The inferior status of women is less obvious in other aspects of employment, where there was much higher respect for male only occupations; women's employment, such as nursing, did not command the same respect as male-only positions.

Where both men and women were employed in jobs, such as teaching, there was a real fear among male workers that women's labour would be used to undercut men's wages. The prevailing attitudes towards the poor also reflected on those who worked among them; for example, 'the concern that the poor should not be educated above their station led to a belief that teachers, too, should remain appropriately humble'. In fact, a type of hidden agenda operated to limit their economic activity to labour which was unpaid or undervalued. In occupations, such as education, the growing refinement of the female was a manifestation of diminished utility rather than raised status. However, in the later part of the century, women were still expected to do the most onerous men's work, particularly in rural areas, but men would be ridiculed for helping with women's work. Such an attitude accurately reflected Irish society which was divided along rigid gender lines. There was a huge amount of unemployment and underemployment in Ireland as well as arrant snobbery, with reference to particular types of employment. A contempt for trade, for example, was characteristic of the higher classes in Galway,

> that would rather eat the family estates to the bare rocks rather than earn a living, except in the professions.

The poor imitated these 'fugitives from usefulness' in their attitude to trade, generally. However, many poor women ignored this attitude and tried to start small businesses to support themselves and their families, others were caught in a vicious poverty trap, particularly as work available to them was mainly seasonal and irregular. Particularly vulnerable were single females, jobless, unskilled, landless and lacking funds to emigrate. Such women would easily be exploited by family members, particularly if they did not wish to enter state institutions, which were filled with able-bodied, unemployed females who had no other place to go for many decades after the Famine. Where a little charity might have helped women either to set themselves up in trading or allowed them to emigrate, it was noted that there was a hardening of attitudes in Irish society to those in need of assistance:

> Just as people's attitudes to land and marriage were altered by famine and poverty, so also their attitudes to charity were affected.

Married women in families also suffered. As women's earnings declined, more families became destitute and marginalised. Women frequently became the scapegoats of family members who blamed them for worsening economic circumstances, although they were not at fault. In such cases, it is easy to see how they, as victims, were left to do much difficult work. The attitude of some Irishmen in this regard was reprehensible: while they suffered as a result of a repressive and unjust social order, several of them adopted many of the vices of their colonial oppressors, whom they affected to despise. Marx's caricature of the Irish squire as being 'haughty, idle and in debt' could equally be applied to classes of Irishmen of much lower ranks of society. Women and children were the victims of this attitude and they were compelled, through penury and dependency to undertake much difficult work.

After the Famine, women resented the greater resources available to men and their more extensive freedom. However, in small towns men seemed to feel inadequate when they measured themselves against women's economic initiative. More strong women managed to get registered as tenants and owners in towns than in the country. In the disadvantaged Water Lane area of

Galway, Anne Regan was listed as owner of 30 of its 44 properties, and this area was known as Regan's Lane. In Sickeen
Lane, Mary Shaw had a lesser number of properties, although
she had properties in more affluent areas of the city. Smaller
towns, such as Ballymoe, also had some women occupiers.

Some women came to resent the heavy burden of physical
work and some emigrated to escape it, or at least to be paid for it
overseas. Thousands of them forwarded passage money to female
friends and relatives in an attempt to better themselves. One
emigrant Connemara girl wrote as follows:

> I will pay you out next Summer ... it's far better than
> carrying the clieve [*cliabh* = basket carried on the back with
> loads of peat, seaweed, etc.] from Crompán-an-Trá to
> Cruchan-a-Laughta.

The Churches have sometimes been blamed for the low status of
women in Irish society; however, even without church influence
the Irish fiercely believed in a world where gender differences
gave order, balance and rationality to human relations. The
attitudes of the Churches merely reinforced the current views of
the Irish on society rather than initiated this point of view.

In this patriarchal society, there was underlying violence,
much of it domestic, which seems to have been accepted by
society. There was no demand, for instance, to extend the 1853
Aggravated Assaults on Women and Children Act to Ireland and
its provisions did not apply here. In domestic violence cases,
appeals sent to the Lord Lieutenant's office in the latter half of
the century reveal interesting patterns in sentences handed down;
approximately half the appeals by men against sentences for
domestic violence were dealt with favourably. Male defendants
argued in court that women had somehow provoked them into
assaulting them; more and more this related to standards of poor
housekeeping. Many men admitted assaulting their wives but
were excused as their wives were inadequate housekeepers or
homemakers, who did not live up to the norms of society which

demanded that wives be sober and compliant. In many cases, appeals called 'memorials' were sent by wives, who were assaulted, to the Lord Lieutenant; they did not want their husbands to receive jail sentences because of their complete economic dependence on them; there merely wanted the courts to set limits to their behaviour.

By contrast, the Criminal Index Files of 1853–1920 reveal cases where people applied for mitigation of their sentences. The records reveal that most women who had either assaulted or ill treated children were seldom granted a reduction of their sentences, if the woman was fond of drink. This was in direct contrast with the attitude of the courts, which reflected the attitude of society, and is particularly evident in the treatment of alcohol related cases: men's abusive behaviour was often excused by claiming alcohol as an excuse; alcoholic women received harsh sentences. Domestic violence may have been accepted as yet another violent episode in a very violent century; there was no public protest by women, who were quite capable of protesting in other circumstances, including political action, even though they did not have the vote.

Some women took part in election mobs, which allowed the disenfranchised a role in politics; women's role in the bitterly contested 1872 Galway election is of interest: Miss Forrest of the Gort Hotel was described as Sir William Gregory's 'right hand man'. The Claddagh fishwives constituted guards of honour for Michael Morris during the same election campaign. Lady Anne Daly of Galway canvassed the tenants of her husband's estate in Raford and received an anonymous threatening letter denouncing 'her wonderful achievements in canvassing for votes among your peasantry'. Other women took part in bread riots in times of shortages. Some took part in agrarian disturbances and were convicted of the charge of incendiarism. Such action generally reflected resistance to imposed economic changes by communities 'whose structure of economic interdependence encouraged group activity'. In spite of such episodes, however, the ideology of separate spheres limited women's involvement in politics.

One must not forget, however, that many of the most capable people had emigrated leaving behind the caput mortuum of the population – the poor, sick and the imbecile, many of them 'chained with poverty' in an 'apparently incurable residuum of human misery', much of it associated with unemployment and squalid living conditions, despite the overall statistical improvements, a decline in epidemic diseases, improvements in food, clothing and a gradual increase in jobs and wages. The question of accommodation was a major preoccupation: many counted themselves fortunate to have any kind of accommodation however poor in areas, such as West Galway, where several estates were sold by the Encumbered Estates Court. Of the 278 townlands in Ballynahinch barony, 181 or 65.11% of the total were sold, with 58.10% in nearby Moycullen barony, whereas Ross barony had a mere 9.68%. Many of the buyers were Irishmen who had amassed capital in workhouse contracts and were regarded as 'spurious gentry', with most of the faults of their predecessors. For tenants on such estates, the kind of society which the Famine had supposedly destroyed was largely intact for decades to come. A visitor to Aughrisbeag, for instance, noted an estate covered with unrecognised sub-tenants, who paid the middleman double his entire rent. Among them were widows, forsaken wives and young women carrying peat who 'appeared from actual want to be almost reduced to a state of idiocy'. This was not an isolated incident. When Allan Pollock took possession of the Burke Estate at Creggs and Glinsk, he learned that instead of 83 official tenants, there were at that time nearly 600 tenants and a population approaching to nearly 3,000, nearly all the tenants paying £5 or under in rent. Further dislocation was caused by the break-up of clachans, with their community ties, by improving landlords. Tenants came to be 'placed, displaced and replaced', in an attempt to maximise rent rolls by the new owners.

It is little wonder that girls, when they could, emigrated in a calculated pursuit of economic betterment. Literacy and the advent of the 'American letter' pointed to a second chance in life

27: Aran travellers from Inishmore

for them and marriage was seen, in many instances, as an obstacle to material success:

> More than any other single factor, it was the difference between the desire and reality and the awesome difficulty of translating ambition into actual achievement, which prompted the rejection by so many Irish men and women.

For women who stayed in Ireland, their role was generally seen as one of 'submissive passivity'; this was certainly the role prescribed by society for the unmarried girl, particularly if unemployed, a deserted wife, an agnostic or non-practising Christian, for whom the latter half of the century was miserable.

The growth of feminism (which has always developed in resistance to sex roles which stunt women's development as responsible adult human beings who direct their own lives to ends of their own choosing) was very slow in Ireland, where many women accepted the status quo for women, however reprehensible. Change in the lives of women came very slowly, often through efforts made by women themselves to obtain better education and to provide employment. In fact, there were no watersheds that fundamentally altered the nature of woman's place in society or that radically changed their economic or social contribution to society during the century.

Sources

Full titles are given here of relevant official reports, such as the Poor Inquiry (1835) which contains Appendices A-H, each dealing with specific aspects of the lives of the poor:

Poor Inquiry, rep.I: First report from commissioners for inquiring into the condition of the poor in Ireland, with Appendices and supplements H.C. 1835 (369), xxxii, pt. I.

CNE: Commissioners of National Education. References have been made to several of its reports.

Devon Commission (1844) examines the occupation of land in Ireland.

Griffith's Valuation: Return of the names and proprietors and the area and valuation of all properties in the several counties of Ireland: H.C. 1876 (412) lxxx.

Powis Commission: Royal Commission of Inquiry into Primary Education (Ireland) 1870.

Saunder's Newsletters: A series of newsletters from correspondents throughout Ireland since 1827 and published in book form in 1862.

Transactions: Transactions of the Central Relief Committee of the Society of Friends during the Famine in Ireland in 1846 and 1847.

Abbott, Edith, *Historical aspects of immigration*, Chicago (1926), pp. 662–5

de Beaumont G., *L'Irlande*, Brussels (1839) Vol. I, pp. 220–35 translated by David Thomson

Blackstone, Wm., *Commentaries on the Law of England*, London (1826), p. 432

Blake, Mrs., *Letters from the Irish Highlands*, London (1825) p. 310 et passim

Bicheno, J., *Ireland and its economy: being the result of observations made in a tour throughout the country in the autumn of 1829*, London (1830)

Bourke, Joanna, *Husbandry to housewifery: women, economic change and housework in Ireland 1890–1914*, Oxford (1993), pp. 152–57, 264–75

Carlyle, T., *Reminiscences of my Irish journey in 1849*, London (1882), pp. 183–9

Cloakey, R.F.,'Irish female emigration from workhouses' in *Journal of the Statistical and Social Inquiry Society of Ireland*, Dublin (1862), p. 418, 428

Corish, P., *The Irish Catholic experience*, Dublin (1985), pp. 166, 179

Cullen, L.M.,' Incomes, social classes and economic growth' in T.M. Dickson and D. Devine (eds.), *Ireland and Scotland 1600–1800*, Edinburgh (1983), p. 258

Devon Commission (1844), pp. 131, 349, 389, 470, 474, 550–5

Diner, Hasia, *Erin's daughters in America: Irish immigrant women in the nineteenth century*, Baltimore and London (1983), pp. xiv, 12

Dutton, Hely, *A statistical and agricultural survey of the county of Galway*, London (1824), pp. 200, 301, 340–3, 354–5, 358–9

Edwards, Dudley R., *An atlas of Irish history*, London (1973), p. 205

Fitzpatick, D., 'A share of the Honeycomb: education, emigration and Irishwomen' in *Contnuity and Change*, Vol. I, No. 2 (1986), pp. 217–34

— 'The modernisation of the Irish female' in P. O'Flanagan et al. (eds.), *Rural Ireland: modernisation and change 1600–1900*, Cork (1987), p. 164

Forbes, John, *Memorandums made in Ireland in the Autumn of 1852* London (1853), vol. I, p. 232

Gibson, Ed., 'Employment of women in Ireland' in *Journal of the Dublin Statistical Society* (April 1962), pp. 133, 141–2

Hardiman, J., *The history of the town and county of Galway*, Dublin (1820), pp. 292–4

Harrington, J.P. (ed.), *The English traveller in Ireland, and the Irish through five centuries*, Dublin (1991), p. 211

Hayden, Tom (ed.), *Irish hunger, personal reflections on the legacy of the famine*, Dublin (1991), pp. 271–94

Hyland, A., 'Church and State in Irish Primary Education', *Irish Independent I.N.T.O. Supplement*, Dublin 18 October (1993), p. 8.

Inglis, H.D., *Ireland in 1834, Parts I and II*, 5th edition, London (1938), pp. 87, 240

Kinealy, C. *This great calamity: the Irish Famine 1845–52*, Dublin (1994), pp. 62–90

Kohl, J.G., *Ireland*, London (1843), p. 42

Lecky, cited in J.Warburton et als. *History of the city of Dublin*, London (1818) p. 00

Lee, J., *The modernisation of Irish society 1848–1918*, Dublin (1973), p. 4

— 'Women and the Church since the Famine' in M. MacCurtain and D O'Corrain (eds), *Womem and Irish society*, Dublin (1978) 36–9.

Luddy, M. *Women in Ireland (1800–1918)*, Cork (1995), p. 160

— *Women and philanthropy in nineteenth–century Ireland*, Cambridge (1995), p. 214

— 'Women and politics in nineteenth-century Ireland' in M. Valiulis and M. O'Dowd (eds), *Women in Irish history: essays in honour of Margaret MacCurtain*, Dublin (1997)

Miller, D.W, 'Irish Catholics and the Great Famine' in *Journal of Social History* (1979), vol. 9, pt. I., p. 80

Nolan, Janet, 'The great famine and women's emigration' in E.M. Crawford (ed.), *The hungry stream* (1997), pp. 61–71

O'Gráda, C., *Ireland before and after the famine: explorations in economic history (1800–1925)*, Manchester (1992), pp. 180–1

Osborne, S.G.O., *Gleanings in the West of Ireland*, London (1950), pp. 98, 192, 242

O'Sullivan, James, *The education of Irish Catholics 1778–1831*, Belfast (1959), pp. 35–7, 70–80

O'Tuathaigh, G.,'The role of women in Ireland under the new English order' in M. MacCurtain and D. O'Corrain (eds), *Women and Irish society*, Dublin (1978), p. 35

— *Ireland before the Famine 1798–1848*, Dublin (1990), pp. 35–8

Oxley, Deborah, *Convict maids: the forced migration of women to Australia*, Cambridge (1996), p. 226

Revans, John, *Evils of the state of Ireland*, London (1835), pp. 33, 58

Scott, T.C., *Connemara after the famine: journal of a survey of the Martin estate in 1853*, Dublin (1995), p. 16

Sommerville, A., *Letters from Ireland during the famine*, ed. Snell, Dublin (1994), pp. 67, 182

Strauss, E., *Irish nationalism and British democracy*, London (1951), p. 118

de Tocqueville, A., *Journeys to England and Ireland*, ed. J.P. Mayer, London (1958), p. 118

Torrens, W.M., *Plan of an association in aid of the Irish Poor Law*, London (1838), pp. 6–9

Tranter, N.L., *Population and society 1750–1940*, London (1985), p. 102

Trevelyan, Wm., *The Irish crisis*, London (1849), pp. 2–8

Tuke, James Hack, *Reports and papers relating to the proceedings of the committee of Mr Tuke's Fund for assisting emigration from Ireland during the years 1882–84* (London) 1880, p. 157

Wakefield, Ed., *An account of Ireland, statistical and political*, 2 volumes, London (1812), vol. II, p. 767

Whelan, Kevin, 'Pre- and Post-Famine landscape change' in C. Poirteir, (ed.) *The Great Irish Famine* Dublin (1995), pp. 22–6

Wilde, Sir Wm., *Irish popular superstitions*, Dublin (1852), pp. 91–2

Notes

PAGE 9   'landlords and moneylenders': Strauss (1951), p. 118

PAGE 10   'house and gardens': Kohl (1857), p. 42.

PAGE 10   'all seasons of the year': Appendix D, p. 243.

PAGE 10   'underemployed labour': Whelan (1995), pp. 22–6.

PAGE 13   'by the people': Curwen (1818) cited in Harrington (1991), p. 211.

PAGE 14   'lazy wretches, who prefer beggary to work': de Beaumont (1839) cited in N. Mansergh, *The Irish question, 1840–1921*, London (1965), p. 24. De Beaumont thought the Irish slothful, deceitful, intemperate and violent. Foreign observers especially accounted for Irish poverty in terms of the people's laziness: they were indolent, they made no effort, they neglected their land, they neglected their dwellings and they neglected their personal appearance. For a fuller discussion of this topic, see C. Maxwell *Country and town in Ireland under the Georges* London (1940), pp. 127–8 and Bertram Hutchinson 'On the study of non-economic factors in Irish economic development' in *Irish Economic and Social Review* 1:4, July 1970, pp. 513–9.

PAGE 19   'other female work': Powis Commission (1870), Vol. XVIII, p. 45.

PAGE 21   'not husband and wife': Commissioners to Burke, P.R.O.I., (Public Record Office of Ireland) vol. 4, 12 August 1843.

PAGE 21   'unencumbered with families': Burke to Commissioners, P.R.O.I., vol. 4, July 1843.

PAGE 21   'unemployment and destitution': 1851 Census, p. 557.

PAGE 21   'choke up every thoroughfare': Osborne (1850), p. 49.

PAGE 22   'their families and communities': Diner (1983), p. xiv.

PAGE 23   'subject, subsidiary and restricted': O'Tuathaigh (1978), p. 35.

PAGE 23   'confined by tradition': Lee (1978), p. 37 et passim.

PAGE 23   'a father, husband or a son': Gibson (1862), p. 141.

PAGE 23   'payment of annuities': Blake Family Papers.

PAGE 23 'is absolutely vested in': Blackstone (1826), p. 432.

PAGE 23 'forced to succumb': Dutton (1824), p. 200.

PAGE 24 'unemployment they needed': Fitzpatrick (1987), p. 164.

PAGE 24 'arithmetic and book-keeping': Gibson (1862), p. 142.

PAGE 24 'redundant in nineteenth century Ireland': Fitzpatrick (1987), p. 164.

PAGE 26 'of great interest': Hardiman (1820), pp. 292–4.

PAGE 28 'all in darkness': Wilde (1852), pp. 91–2.

PAGE 42 'on the men': Bicheno cited in Appendix H, Part II, p. 19.

PAGE 52 'hasten the process': Dutton (1824), p. 141.

PAGE 53 'many additional ones': Revans (1835), p. 58.

PAGE 53 'to enforce obedience': O'Grada (1992), p. 180.

PAGE 54 'indifference to all consequences': Appendix A, p. 363.

PAGE 55 'go to ruin': McCulloch, cited in O'Grada (1992), p. 181.

PAGE 56 'of his parents' estate': Diner (1983), pp. xiv, 12.

PAGE 56 'marriage prospects': Lee (1973), p. 38.

PAGE 58 'for the dispensation':Corish(1985), p. 179.

PAGE 58 'average age at marriage': Lee (1973), p. 4.

PAGE 58 'postponement of marriage': Miller (1979), p. 82.

PAGE 60 'die or do worse': Gibson (1862), p. 141.

PAGE 60 'the troubles of life': Blake (1825), pp. 310 et passim

PAGE 61 'side of the water': Inglis (1838), p. 87.

PAGE 70 'poteen was': Dutton (1824), p. 367.

PAGE 71 'positively worse off': Appendix A, p. 117.

PAGE 72 'salt leaves in return': Appendix A, p.115.

PAGE 74 'nursery of vice': *Famine Ireland*, vol. IV, p. 94.

PAGE 82 'made in this direction': Osborne (1850), p. 242.

PAGE 83 'a young substitute': Dutton (1824), p. 521.

PAGE 84 'the rustic festivities': Wilde (1852), p. 15.

PAGE 84 'sheep in their flocks': Webb, cited in *Freeman's Journal*, 2 August 1847.

PAGE 85 'in the Poor House': *Galway Packet*, 6 April 1854.

PAGE 85 'divisions of the nation': Lecky (1878), p. 611.

PAGE 89 'to secure it': *Galway Vindicator*, 30 October 1850.

PAGE 90 'may be sent': Cloakey (1863), p. 418 et passim.

PAGE 95 'practical knowledge of': CNE (1853) Book on Needlework, Marlborough Street.

PAGE 97 'instruction of the children': B.P.P. 1831–34, vol. V., p. 327.

PAGE 100 'the French *ouvroirs*': O'Sullivan (1959), p. 80.

PAGE 104 'were as follows': *Thom's Directory* (1857), p. 511.

PAGE 106 'of their pupils': *Irish Times*, 23 January 1871.

PAGE 106 'was founded in 1879': Hyland (1993), p. 8.

PAGE 109 'hold 80,000–100,000 people': Kinealy (1994), p. 62.

PAGE 118 'them within reach': *Galway Vindicator*, 9 August 1849.

PAGE 120 'fearful vault': Tuke (1847), p. 195.

PAGE 121 'propagation of cholera': Appendix A, p. 287.

PAGE 124 'the ruined cabin': Abbott (1926), pp. 662–5.

PAGE 124 'wherever it exists': *The Times*, 12 February 1880.

PAGE 125 'middle-class Irishwomen': Luddy (1995), p. 214.

PAGE 131 'Among these migrants': Strauss (1951), pp. 82–3.

PAGE 144 'the Board of Guardians': *Galway Standard*, 15 March, 1843.

PAGE 148 'male-only positions': Luddy (1995) p. 160.

PAGE 148 'in the professions': Sommerville (1994), p. 67.

PAGE 154 'Irish men and women': Tranter (1985), p. 102.

PAGE 154 'society during the century': Luddy (1995), p. xxvii.

List of Illustrations

1: Eyre Square, the 'heart of Galway': a busy Fair Day scene   11

2: A map of Galway showing the baronies, after Edwards,
An atlas of Irish history   12

3: A Galway fishwife   16

4: An ass heavily laden with seaweed (*feamainn*), which
was valued as a fertilizer   17

5: 'Rags seem the refuse of a sheep' (Sir Walter Scott).
Foreign visitors frequently commented on the poor
quality of Irish clothing.   20

6: Plan of a prosperous cabin in the Aran Islands   27

7: Connemara cabin (1843) with 'original Connaught pig'
(Hall), a tall pig, which was doomed to extinction:
pigs were swept away in cholera epidemics   27

8: An Aran Islands scene   30

9: An eviction in progress   31

10: The aftermath of eviction   32

11: A dispossessed family. Note the *duidin* or clay pipe,
widely used by women at that time   32

12: Animals were also famine victims: horses were eaten
or died as a result of malnutrition as available oats was
eaten by humans.   35

13: Connemara women in a variety of dress (1880)   37

14: A tuirne mór or large spinning wheel frequently
formed part of a dowry   39

15: 'Important business belongs to women' (John Gregg,
28 February 1856). Note the *cliabh* (clieve) or back
basket carried by the women who carried out the most
difficult tasks.   41

16: 'Dúirt bean liom': trade and gossip at the Spanish
Arch, Galway.   45

17: 'Sunday best' clothes at Eyre Square, Galway   59
18: 'Going to the market', Salmon Weir Bridge, Galway   69
19: Working woman walking along the canal between New Road and Dominick Street, Galway   69
20: 'Offering for sale their beautiful Connemara stockings of every variety of hue and more especially red' (Thackeray)   71
21: Garumna Island: dinner on Indian meal supplied by a relief committee.   111
22: Augusta Crofton at Clonbrock House, May 1866   126
23: A woman in lace cap and plaid shawl at Clonbrock House   127
24: Drawingroom, Clonbrock House   128
25: Clonbrock House   128
26: Traditional housing at Dogfish Lane in the Claddagh, beside the Claddagh Church   135
27: Aran travellers from Inishmore   153

LIST OF ACKNOWLEDGEMENTS

Ills 1, 21–5 are courtesy of the National Library, Dublin.

Ill. 2, is after the 'Map of Connaught' in R. Dudley Edwards: *An atlas of Irish history*

Ills. 3, 4, 8, 14, 16, 17, 20, 27 are courtesy of the National Museum, Dublin.

Ills. 5, 7, 9–13, 15 are courtesy of the *Illustrated London News*.

Ills. 18–19 are courtesy of the Frost Collection, Galway County Library.

Ill. 26 is courtesy of the County Library, Galway.

Ill. 6 is after Haddon and Browne, 'The ethnography of the Aran Islands'.

Index

Abbott, E. 124
Abbeyknockmoy 77
Act of Union 86
Aggravated Assaults on Women
    and Children Act 150
agriculture
    changing pattern of 22
    subsistence 9
Ahascragh 31, 79
America 84
annuities 23
Aran Islands 26, 47, 67, 77
Ardrahan 87
Ardfry 138
Army Commissariat 125
Athenry 39
Aughrim 40
Aughrisbeg 152
Augustinians 118
Augustinian Christian
    Doctrine Society 118
Australia 64

Ballinakill (Connemara) 45, 69
Ballinakill (East Galway) 48, 98
Ballinglass 137
Ballinasloe 13, 25, 30, 87, 93, 97,
    116, 144
Ballymacward 67, 130
Ballynahinch 65, 119

Barna 36, 52, 72, 80
Barrett, Bridget 140
Beagh 26
begging 21, 48
    'half begging' 71
Beaumont de, Gustave 25
Berridge, Lord 31
Bicheno, J. 42
Bird, Golding 89
Blackstone, Sir Wm. 24
Blake Family papers 23
Blake, Mr 69, 72
Blake, Mrs 81
Boards of Guardians 116, 144
Bouchier, Catherine 142
Boughill (Crown estate) 122
Boula 93
Bourke, Joanna 24
Britain 138
British Relief Association 39, 102,
    117
Burke Estate 152
Burke, J. 21

cabins (see housing) 25–36
Calcutta 118
Camus 36
Canada 90, 122
cannibalism 120
Carlyle, Thomas 25, 122

Carr, Mary 70
Cashla 110
Castlefrench 116
Castlegar (Ahascragh) 30, 31
Castlefrench 116
Castlehacket 103
Castlekirke 81
Castletaylor 79
Catholic Church
    aid 124
    women 124
Census 1831 59
Census 1841 13
Census 1851 13, 18, 22
Census 1861 147
Census 1871 13, 23
Census 1881 60
Chicago 118
child mortality 23
cholera   29, 34, 67
church registers 79
clachans 34, 35
Claddagh 23, 26, 28, 37, 56, 65,
    82, 95, 120, 151
Clancarty, Lord 31,45
Clanricarde, Lord 31
Clare, Barony of 99
Clarenbridge 30, 39
Cleggan 116
Clifden 13, 50, 74, 89, 90, 94, 115,
    118–21
Cloakey, R.F. 90
Clonbrock, Lord 31,33
Clonfert 17, 26, 55, 73, 87
Clonkeen 77, 86
Clontuskert 55,87
Cloonan, Widow 83
clothing:
    'beetling' 38

effects of famine on 38
    materials 36
    poor quality 36
    'troggers' 39
Clougherty, Patrick 140
Coalpark 109
Commissioners of National
    Education (CNE) 19, 93, 104
conacre 45–7, 109, 139
Connacht 116
*Connaught Church Endowment
    Society* 80
Connaught Journal 80
Conneely, Mary 138
Connemara 13, 26, 34, 48, 150
Connor, Bridget 136
Connor, Mary 143
Convict Referennce books 142–3
Corish, P. 58
Coole 30
Cork 137
Cosgriff, Thomas 140
cottage industry 10
Craddon, Eleanor 141
Craughwell 30
credit 'on time' 49
Creggs 152
crime
    against property 136
    against the person 136
    against behaviour 136
    arson 141
    theft – food, fuel 136
    incendiarism 141, 151
    incidence 145
    infanticide 138
    rape cases 142
    rural (agrarian) 137–8; 139–41,
        151
    disturbances 138, 151

Criminal Index Files 151
Criminal Law Amendment
    Act 139
Curwen, J. 13

Dallas, Revd A R 81
Danesfield 31
D'Arcy, Mrs 70
D'Arcy, Revd John 81
Daly, Lady Anne 151
Derry, Dr (Bishop of Clonfert) 81
Devon Commission 28
Diner, Hasia 22,56
disease:
    in cabins, 29–30, 47
    cholera 29, 67
    smallpox 29
    measles 29
    scrofula 121
    scurvy 121
    typhus 46, 121
domestic service 19
Dominican Convent (Taylor's
    Hill) 95, 96
Dominican Fathers (Claddagh)
    39, 85
    schools 118
Dominican Fathers (Esker) 39
Donamon 130
Donohue, Celia 141
dowries 54, 56
    non-payment of 56 et passim
Doyle, Bishop James (JKL) 54
Dublin Castle 125
Duniry 77
Dunmore 13
Dunsandle, Lord 31
Dutton, Hely 23, 25, 51, 82, 147

Education (see teachers and
    schools) 85–107
Edwards, Dudley R. 12
emigration (composite entry)
    assisted emigration schemes
        122–3, 133
    migration 129
    seasonal 130
    as subsistence stragegy 131
    step-wise migration 132
employment 15–24
Encumbered Estates Act 35, 80,
    114
Encumbered Estates Court 133,
    152
England 46, 131–2, 145
Errismore 51
Esker 39
evictions 116, 137
Eyrecourt 13

Famine, Great 10, 43, 109, 123, 124
farming
    subsistence 15
Farrell, Honor 141
fever (see disease) 120–1
fever hospitals 115
Finn, Rev. Mark 72
fishing 19
Fitzpatrick, David 24, 102
Forbes, John 70
Folan, Fr 85, 118
food
    prices 43
    maize 43
    'truck system' 45
    shortages 46
    substitutes 122

Ford, Widow 73
Forrest, Miss 151
Forster, Wm. 117, 119, 120
Franciscans 118
Freeman's Journal 120
French, Mary Anne 143–4

Galway
  assizes 136
  civil ejections 137
Galway (City) 78
  Bohermore 25, 29
  Model School 106
  St. Nicholas 64, 97, 123
Galway Advertiser 96
Galway Packet 85
Galway Patriot 94
Galway Standard 144
Galway Vindicator 20, 41, 109,
  117–20
Garbally 30
Garumna Island 110
Gerrard, John 116
Gerrard, Mrs 137
Gibson, Ed. 60
Gleanings in the West of Ireland 89
gombeenman 49
Gort 13, 30, 41, 92, 116
Grand Jury cess 110
Gregory Clause 73, 114–16
Gregory, Sir William 151
Griffin, Celia 120

Hall, Mr and Mrs S.C 20
Hardiman, J 28
Hardis, Capt. 26
Hayden, Tom 145
Headford 13, 25, 48, 65, 69, 121
Heathcote, Dr George 47

Heavy, Catherine 137
hedge schools 100
Holland, Captain 123
homelessness 35, 36, 116
housing
  building materials 26
  cabins 25
  Claddagh 23–6
  Third Class 33
  Fourth Class 33
  superior housing 30, 31
  temporary housing
    (scailpeens) 35
Huxters 21, 70
Hyland, A. 106
Hynes, Margaret 141

Illustrated London News 112
indolence (see note on
  idleness)
infanticide 60
Inglis, H.D. 28, 147
inheritance
  impartible 55
  primogeniture 56
  ultimogeniture 56
  effects of Famine 55
'in hold' 48
Innisboffin 47, 50, 122
Irish Church Education Society
  98
Irish Education Act (1892)
  102
Irish Relief Committee 119
Irish Society for Irish Church
  Missions 80
Irish Times 106
Irvilloughter (crown estate) 122–3,
  133

Jackson, Oliver 109
Jones, Mary 143

Keady, Mary 83
Kelly, Connor 109
Kenny, Fr Francis 83
Kilbecanty 28
Kilcreest 48
Kilcolgan 87
Kilconnell 25,63
Kilcooley 93
Kilcummin 48
Kildare Commission 50, 62–4, 70,
    87
Kildare Place Society 86, 91, 92
Kilglass 130
Killanin 26
Killeries 72
Killimor 26
Kilkerrin 101
Killoran 26
Kilmacduagh 28, 76
Kilnalahan 77
Kiltartan 87
Kinealy, C. 109
Kinvara 35
Kohl, J. 36

Land League 125
landlords 9, 31, 35, 45, 50
    absentee 50, 69
    proselytising 82
    resident 31, 50
Lecky 85
Lee, J.J. 23, 56–8
Lettermore 110
Letters from the Irish Highlands 95
London 100
Londonderry, Lord 137

London Hibernian Society 86
Loughbeg 138
Lough Cutra Castle 30
Loughrea 26, 50, 89, 101, 144
Luddy, Maria 125, 154
Lynch, Mark 96
Lyons Honoria 93

McCulloch, J.I. 55
MacHale, Archbishop John 74, 98
Magdalen Asylum 79–80
maize (Indian corn) 43–4, 49,
    110, 114, 125
Mannion, Thomas 140
Mansion House Committee 110,
    119, 125
Marlborough, Duchess of 24
    Committee of 125
marriage:
    prospects 23, 61
    youthful, improvident, 53
    age at marriage 54
    marriage fees 57, 58
    'out of dock' 66
    non-marriage 59
    postponed marriage 59
    provision for 55
    decline 123
Marriage Law Amendment Act
    57
Marx, Karl 149
Maxey, Miss 100
Mayo 47, 111, 137
Melbourne 119
Mercy Sisters 78–80, 117
Midas (ship) 121
Miller, D.W. 58
Miller, Mr (Blantyre) 51
Monaghan, Elizabeth 142

Monivea 31, 64, 130

Morris, Michael 151

Mountbellew 25,116

Moycullen 63, 66, 70, 78, 83, 99, 152

Moygownagh (Co. Mayo) 69

Moyne Park 31

Moyrus 7

Munster 116

Napoleonic Wars 10, 45

Navigation Acts 113

Netterfield, Miss 86

New York 118

Nicholson, Asenath 13

Nolan, Janet 52, 154

Nuisance and Disease Prevention Acts 34

O'Donnell family 118

O'Donnell, Count Maurice 118

O'Grada, C. 53

Omey Island 26, 37, 65, 69

Oranmore 47

Osborne, S.G.O. 21, 81–2, 89, 90

O'Tuathaigh, G. 23

Oughterard 69, 112

ouvroirs 100

Oxley, Deborah 147

Page Hanify, Michael J. 119

pawning 39, 50

Pazzi de, Sr. Mary 118

peasantry 53

Peel, Robert 110

Peel's 'brimstone' 110

Perry, James 119

Pim, Jonathan 119

Pollock, Alan 152

Poor House (see Workhouse)

Poor Law 65, 73

Poor Law Acts (1847) 114

Poor Law Commisioners 21, 91, 115, 144

Poor Law Guardians 90, 96, 116

Portumna 100

Post Office 19

potatoes:

   prices 43

   varieties 46

   diseases 109

Poverty Commission 54, 67

Powis Commission 87, 93, 101

Presentation Convent Schools 94

Presentation Sisters 39, 117–18

proselytism 82

prostitution 74, 136

Quakers (see Society of Friends)

Quinn, Anne 141

rack rents 45

Raford 151

Regan, Anne 150

Regan's Lane 150

Relief Extension Act (1847) 130 et passim

religion:

   Catholic 75 *et passim*

   Church of Ireland 75

   tithes 75, 138

   tithe war 75

   church attendance 76

   stations 76, 84

   devotions 77

   priests' dues 78

   fall off in practice 83–4

religion: *(cont.)*
    Devotional Revolution 84
    religious instruction 84
    schools 97 *et passim*
Revans John 53
Revenue police 139
Rinolfi, Fr 118
Robins, Widow 70
Rome 118
Roo 35
Ross 63, 99, 152
Roundstone 140
Royal Commission on Education
    100
Ruananule (Roundstone) 140
Ruane, Bridget 138
Russell, Lord John 110

St Cleran's (Craughwell) 30
St George, Mr 68, 121
St George, Mrs 68
St John's (New Brunswick) 121
Sanitary Act 34
Saunders Newsletters 34, 51
Scannell, Widow 73, 74
schools
    hedge 100
    Irish language 98–100
    superior 87
    Powis Commission 87
    private 19, 87
    workhouse 88
    Loughrea 88
    standards 88
    Model Schools 92
    Monitor system 92–4
    ouvroirs 100
    hidden curriculum 97
    Sunday schools 97

    enrolments 101
    attainments 103 *et passim*
    salaries 104–6
Scotland 42, 46, 51
Scott, Sir Walter 70
scullogues 49
Second Reformation 82
Shaw, Mary 150
Sickeen Lane 150
Society of Friends 116–17
    (Quakers) 39, 116, 117
Soup Kitchen Act
    (Burgoyne's Act) 112
Soup Kitchen Scheme 114
Sommerville, A. 148
Spiddal 35, 112
Stanley, Chief Secretary 108
'standings' 21
stockings 18
Strzelecki, Count 39
Sub-Letting Act 15

Taylor family 79
Taylor, Jane 79
Teachers
    salaries 105
    training 92
    Marlborough St. 92
    Normal Establishments 92
textile industries 9
Tiernascragh 26
The Times 116
Thorngate, James 116
Tocqueville de, A. 140
Torrens 15
transportation 138, 141
transportation registers 140, 141
Tranter, N.L. 154
Trevelyan, C.E. 46

Troggers 39

Tuam 13, 26, 86, 109, 116, 118, 122, 138
  archdiocese of 98
Tuke, James Hack 120
Tully 28
Twinnings, Francis 116
Tyrone House 30

underemployment 15, 21
underwages 48
unemployment 15, 21
  disguised 9
  structural 9
  long term effects 22
  underemployment 21
unmarried mothers
  marriage prospects 61
  legal processes 61–3
  provision for 62
unmarried men 59
USA (America) 117, 123–4, 131, 145, 147
  grain imports from 131

vagrancy 139, 142
vagrants, discharge of 142–3
vagrant women 139
vestry cess 64
The Victorian (Melbourne) 119
violence 23, 139–40; 150–1

wages 44, 45, 111, 113
  under-wages 48
Wakefield, Ed. 147
Wales 145

Walshe, Paddy 28
Ward, Anne 144
Water Lane 149
Webb, Richard 84
Western Argus 142
Whelan, Kevin 22–6
widows 60
widow's holding 69
Widows and Orphans Asylum 72
Widows and Orphans Refuge 125
widowers 74
  rates of remarriage 74
Wilde, Sir Wm. 28, 49, 83
women, role of
  agricultural work, 15
  employment, 18
  female work, 19
  domestic service 19
  role of 134, 141
  philanthropy 125
workhouses
  capacity 109
  Clifden 88–90
  Galway 45, 90, 123
  Loughrea 89
  Infirmary 20
  schools 88–9
  conditions 114
  auxiliary 114
  as refuges 125
Woodlawn 25

York 131
Yorkshire 118